The War in Korea: 1950-1953

On the morning of June 25, 1950, the vanguard of ninety thousand North Korean soldiers plunged south into the Republic of South Korea. Striking with great precision, the Communist North Korean divisions had little difficulty overwhelming the surprised and outnumbered defenders.

The United Nations organization, pledged to defend all nations from aggression, could not ignore this wanton invasion. Immediately the U.N. Security Council called an emergency session, and a few days later the United States began to rush troops and supplies to embattled South Korea. Other member nations also quickly dispatched troops and material. For the first time in history troops of a world organization were acting as a "police force" to fight an aggressor nation.

In *The War in Korea* Robert Leckie presents an authentic and lucid account of an unusual conflict which was fought on two battlefields—across the rugged Korean terrain, where troops met in bloody combat, and around the conference tables, where truce teams engaged in grueling negotiations to bring about a peace.

by Robert Leckie

illustrated with Photographs and Maps

RANDOM HOUSE: NEW YORK

the war in Korea

1950-1953

Grateful acknowledgment is made to *Life* Magazine for permission to use on page 101 the quotation from *Memoirs* by Harry S. Truman, Vol. II, *Years of Trial and Hope,* © 1956 Time Inc.

Photograph credits: Eastfoto, pages 104, 109; Gazet van Antwerpen via U.N., page 37 (bottom); U.S. Marine Corps via Defense Department, page 92; United Nations, pages 28, 34, 160–161; United Press International, pages ii–iii, 11, 14, 31, 77, 96 (bottom); U.S. Air Force, page 111; U.S. Army, pages 43, 83, 96 (top), 132, 165; U.S. Army via United Nations, pages 37 (top), 119, 128; U.S. Navy via United Nations, pages 146, 148; U.S. Navy via Wide World, pages 57, 89; Wide World, pages 22, 26, 46, 47, 51, 53, 61, 63, 73, 102, 118, 123, 127, 137, 139, 151, 154. Front Endpaper: U.S. Marine Corps via Defense Department. Back Endpaper: Wide World.

COVER: UNITED PRESS INTERNATIONAL

 Published in New York by Random House, Inc., and simultaneously in Toronto, Canada, by Random House of Canada, Limited. Manufactured in the United States of America

Designed by Jane Byers

Library of Congress catalog card number: 63-18287

5 366

This title was originally catalogued by the Library of Congress as follows:

Leckie, Robert.

The war in Korea, 1950–1953. New York, Random House [1963]

173 p. illus., ports., maps. 22 cm. (World landmark books, W-57)

Bibliography: p. 167–168.

1. Korean War, 1950–1953—Juvenile literature. I. Title.

Full name: Robert Hugh Leckie.

DS918.L39 951.9 63—18287

Lib. Ed.: ISBN: 0-394-90557-1

For Geoffrey,
Joan,
and David Leckie

Contents

MAPS

The War in Korea: 1950-1953

The U.N. Wins Its First Battle

1

On the night of June 27, 1950, four sleek blue torpedo boats put out of the port of Wonsan in Communist North Korea and roared south through the Sea of Japan.

They were headed for a small harbor captured by Communist North Korean army forces during the sneak invasion of South Korea only two days before. Once there, the mission of the torpedo boats would be to give protection to ten small North Korean freighters which were busy bringing soldiers and supplies to the port.

But on July 2nd, this North Korean "fleet" was intercepted by the first United Nations "navy" in history. On that date, the United States and British cruisers *Juneau* and *Jamaica,* with the little British frigate *Blue Swan,* opened battle with the communist craft.

At the first United Nations salvo, one of the enemy torpedo boats blew up and another was set on fire and began to sink. The other two fled. One ran up on the shore, where it was later destroyed at leisure. And the remaining boat zig-zagged toward the open sea, successfully dodging shells hurled by the pursuing *Blue Swan.*

Then the American cruiser *Juneau* steamed over to the port of Chumunjim, to which the ten little North Korean freighters had scurried for safety. There she opened fire with her big eight-inch guns. Seven of the enemy ships were sunk, while the other three took cover behind a big breakwater where they could not be hit.

The first sea engagement between a communist navy and the vessels of the United Nations had ended in a smashing victory for the U.N. The world's first experiment in what is called "collective security" had survived the fiery test of battle.

How the War Began

2

The "collective security" which brought the United Nations into war with communism was merely an agreement among freedom-loving peoples to band together to fight armed aggression wherever it might arise. Such aggression arose first in Korea, and to understand what happened there during the war of 1950–1953 it is important to know something of the history of that unhappy little land.

Korea is a peninsula extending from the Asian

mainland for about 500 to 600 miles in length and from 90 to 200 miles in width. Although this tiny country does not appear to cover much of the earth's surface, it has been said that she would cover it all if you flattened out her mountains. For Korea is actually a great rugged mountain range jutting out into the sea. Because of her mountainous terrain, and a climate that blazes and freezes by turns, Korea proved to be one of the most miserable places imaginable for fighting a war. Nor did the extreme poverty of her people and their unsanitary habit of fertilizing crops with human dung make military operations any easier.

Strangely enough, this Land of the Morning Calm, as it is often called, has always been fought over. Why? Because she is surrounded by powerful neighbors—Russia, China, and Japan—each wanting to possess her for selfish reasons. On the north, along the vast Yalu River, Korea has a long border with China. To the northeast there is a brief fifteen-mile border with Siberia, which is part of Soviet Russia. And across the Sea of Japan, a distance of approximately

KOREA:
1950-53
MANCHURIA
Chosan
YALU RIVER
CHOSIN
RESERVOIR
Yudam-ni
Hagaru-ri
Koto-ri
Chinhung-ni
Iwon
Hungnam
SEA OF JAPAN
Pyongyang
Wonsan
38TH
PARALLEL
Kaesong
Panmunjom
Uijongbu
Seoul
Chumunjim
Inchon
HAN RIVER
Suwon
Osan
Ansong
Pyongtaek
Chonan
Chochiwon
Poun
Yongdong
Taejon
KUM RIVER
NAKTONG RIVER
Taegu
Miryang
Pusan
Koje
YELLOW SEA
KOREA STRAIT
MANCHURIA
U.S.S.R.
KOREA
SEA OF JAPAN
YELLOW SEA
CHINA
JAPAN

125 miles, are the islands of Japan.

Since the end of the Middle Ages, these three powers have collided with one another in Korea. First China had control, then Japan. Next Russia entered the arena, only to be forcibly evicted by the growing sea power of Japan. The Japanese remained in power from 1905 until the end of World War II in 1945. All the while, the poor people of Korea were struggling for their own independence, but they were always put down by one of these three empires.

After the decisive defeat of Japan in 1945, the problem arose: What to do with Korea? President Franklin D. Roosevelt, and after him President Harry S. Truman, had already announced that Korea must be free and independent. The Russian premier, Joseph Stalin, then America's ally against the German Nazis, agreed with this publicly.

But Stalin is also the man who said: "Sincere diplomacy is no more possible than dry water or iron wood." Despite his public declarations, he was already plotting to gain control of Korea. And for this purpose he had trained thirty-six

Koreans who either had been born in Russia or had fought with the Communists in World War II. These men were to be his puppets in the communist state he hoped to establish in Korea. Their leader was a pudgy guerrilla fighter named Kim Sung Chu.

Stalin's and Kim's chance came immediately after the Japanese surrender ending World War II. It was decided, for convenience, that the Americans would disarm the Japanese occupation troops in southern Korea and the Russians would disarm those in the north. The only problem was to establish a line between them. This was solved when Rear Admiral Matthias Gardner, an American, pointed to the 38th Parallel, which cuts Korea almost in two, and said to his Russian colleagues:

"Why not put it there?"

There the boundary went, and the 38th Parallel was to become famous. Though it was only an imaginary line—the 38th degree of north latitude—the Russians quickly turned it into an armed border which divided Korea into two zones.

From their mountain outpost fur-capped officers of the South Korean army look out over the 38th Parallel.

They tore up all railroad tracks directly north of the Parallel, and armed guards patrolled the border, preventing anyone from the south from entering the north. In addition, pudgy Kim Sung Chu was put in power in the city of Pyongyang. Kim told the peasants of North Korea that he was Kim Il Sung, a legendary Korean fighter and leader who had died resisting the Japanese. Few people dared to doubt Kim, for he was quick to silence or kill anyone who opposed him.

South of the Parallel the Americans who had accepted the surrender of the Japanese troops in Seoul found that the Koreans were now beginning to think of them as new oppressors. The Communists had artfully thrown the blame for the division of Korea on the Americans. Many Koreans were unduly affected by the Communists' propaganda, for they had long wanted a free and united country of their own.

Worse, the Koreans saw that the economy of their beloved land was beginning to wither and die. In the past, the 21,000,000 Koreans south of the Parallel had grown the food and fibers needed by the 9,000,000 Koreans who worked in the factories or the hydroelectric plants of the north. But because the Communists had successfully blocked all exchange of goods and services, the Koreans in the north were without food or raw materials. And those of the south had no electric power to light their cities and sometimes no water. This was also blamed on the United States.

Meanwhile, the Communists in the north, advised by Russian military experts, began building a big army. They also continued their sabotage and propaganda efforts against the Americans in the south. By 1947, President Truman had become so alarmed at this that he took the entire Korean problem to the United Nations. The U.N. General Assembly resolved to hold free elections throughout all of Korea. But the Communists in the north, again following Stalin's orders, refused to allow the U.N. election commission to come north of the Parallel.

Even though Soviet Russia was a member of the United Nations, she did not hesitate to thwart the U.N. organization when it tried to give all Koreans the chance to elect their own government. The U.N.-sponsored elections were held only south of the Parallel, and a government was elected with Seoul as the capital city. Fierce old Syngman Rhee became president. Syngman Rhee was a Korean patriot who had opposed the Japanese, and had been tortured and jailed and finally sent into exile.

In reply to this new Republic of Korea, soon

Syngman Rhee

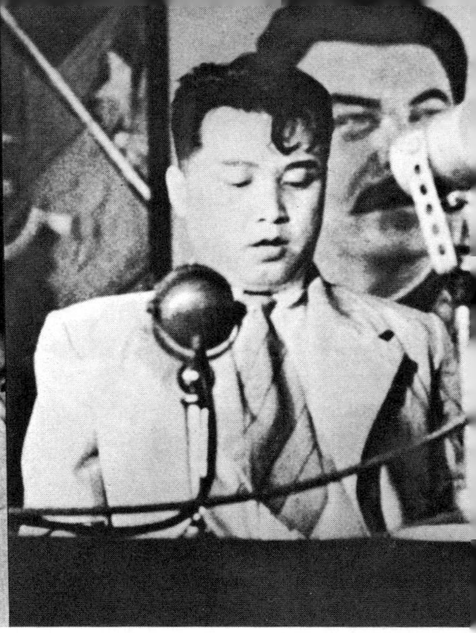

Kim Il Sung

to be known as South Korea, Kim Il Sung held his own mock elections in the north. Then he proceeded to proclaim the establishment of the People's Democratic Republic of Korea, which was called North Korea. Kim's capital was in Pyongyang.

So now unhappy little Korea was truly cut in half. Premier Kim Il Sung in North Korea was a communist puppet dangling at the end of Stalin's string, while President Rhee in South Korea was an elected leader depending on the United Nations and the United States for his support. Thus democracy and communism confronted one another in Korea. It should have been obvious that they would soon collide, but unfortunately the eyes of the world were focused elsewhere.

Since the end of World War II the Communists had been intent on gobbling up the countries of Central Europe. They were able to do this because the American people, as well as the other Allied nations who defeated the Axis, were weary of war and reluctant to start another one. So the Communists were able to strike out on their quest for world domination.

Nearly all of Central Europe fell under communist influence. One by one, Poland, Czechoslovakia, Hungary, Rumania, Bulgaria, Albania, and what is now called East Germany, became communist states controlled by Premier Stalin in Moscow. All of these nations were taken over by the device of undermining their legitimate governments. Then, in Greece and Turkey, the Communists tried force. President Truman quickly authorized a program for aid to Greece and Turkey. Under the leadership of Lieutenant

General James Van Fleet, who would one day command the Eighth Army in Korea, the communist forces were defeated.

Meanwhile, in Korea, the goal of the Communists appeared to be peace. In 1949, with great fanfare, Premier Stalin withdrew his troops from North Korea and called home most of the military experts who had built up the North Korean army. In turn the American forces left South Korea. For its defense the little republic, led by President Syngman Rhee, now relied completely on its own army. The soldiers of this army were nicknamed "ROKs" after the initials of the Republic of Korea. Though advised by American officers, the ROK army was inferior to the communist army in the north. The ROK soldiers were armed only with small arms and outmoded artillery. And unlike the North Korean army they had no tanks or airplanes.

During the same year—1949—that the Russians and Americans were withdrawing from Korea, important events were taking place in nearby China. The Chinese Communists, led by Mao Tse-tung, at last overthrew the Nationalist government of Chiang Kai-shek and drove Chiang and his army from China to the island of Formosa. This conflict, however, was an internal civil war, so outside nations did not believe they had any right to intervene in China. But because force had been used, the United Nations refused to allow Red China to become a member of the world organization.

As a result of Mao Tse-tung's victory, the new communist state of North Korea had communist neighbors all along her northern border: Red China and Red Russia. The time was ripe for the boldest and most lawless move of all: the wanton invasion of the state of South Korea, with its legally elected government.

The attack came during a heavy rainfall early in the morning of June 25, 1950. The only warning given South Korean soldiers all along the 38th Parallel was the thump and crash of mortar shells falling among them, the high peening of bullets, and the hoarse cries of their stricken and dying comrades.

The Communists had thrown off the cloak of concealment. They were relying on naked power.

The Fall of Seoul

3

Even as the vanguard of 90,000 North Korean soldiers and hundreds of tanks plunged into South Korea, Premier Kim Il Sung was announcing to the world that his nation was acting "in self-defense."

In the afternoon of June 25, 1950, Kim made a radio broadcast claiming that "the bandit Syngman Rhee" had attacked North Korea. Kim's nation, according to him, had taken up arms only to defend itself. He did not explain how it was that the "defending" army was at that time ten or twenty miles inside the borders of the "attacking" army. Obviously, contrary to what Kim might say, the invasion of South Korea had been planned well in advance. The communist divisions were striking with great precision down five different invasion routes.

They had almost no difficulty overwhelming the surprised and outnumbered ROKs. Only one small sector on the east coast offered stiff resistance, and this was because the North Koreans there had attacked without tanks. But wherever the big Russian-built T-34 tanks were at work, the South Korean defenses crumbled.

These metal monsters each fired an 85-millimeter cannon and a pair of heavy machine guns. ROK soldiers using 37-millimeter antitank guns or an occasional American bazooka of light caliber just could not stop them. Their shells exploded harmlessly against the sides of the thick-skinned T-34s. The tanks roared down on the South Korean roadblocks, making a mash of the log-and-sandbag barriers. They flushed terrified defenders into full view of the North Korean infantrymen, who came trotting along behind the tanks. Sometimes valiant ROK soldiers rushed a T-34 with explosive charges, but the enemy riflemen cut them down before they could reach the tank.

And so the North Korean charge was sweeping all before it. By nightfall of June 25th, except for that momentary setback in the east, all the North Korean divisions had carried out their missions or even exceeded them. By that time, too, all the nations of the free world realized that they stood on the brink of World War III.

June 25th in Korea was June 24th in the United States, for Korea is east of the international date line and America west of it. Because of this, and also because of the confusion that always attends the outbreak of war, officials in Washington, D.C., did not learn of the Korean crisis until 9:26 the night of Saturday, June 24th. At that time, the following telegram was received at the State Department:

North Korean forces invaded Republic of Korea

> territory at several points this morning.... It would appear from the nature of the attack and the manner in which it was launched that it constitutes an all-out offensive against ROK.
>
> [John J.] Muccio [U.S Ambassador to Seoul]

A half-hour later, the report was in the hands of Secretary of State Dean Acheson, who quickly telephoned President Harry S. Truman, then on vacation at his home town in Independence, Missouri.

"Mr. President," the Secretary said, "I have very serious news. The North Koreans have invaded South Korea." He added that it might be well to request an emergency meeting of the Security Council of the United Nations to press for a cease-fire in Korea. The President agreed, and the session was arranged. It was to take place at two o'clock Sunday afternoon.

In South Korea that following day, June 26th, the ROK army made a desperate attempt to save Seoul, which lay fifty miles south of the 38th Parallel. The ROK leaders wanted to hold the highway city of Uijongbu, about twenty miles above Seoul. If they could do this, the

enemy tanks would be denied the road to Seoul.

Two ROK divisions attempted to stop the tanks. But once again they had no weapons powerful enough. Worse, there was an argument between the ROK generals, and one of them refused to move his division into place as he was ordered. Thus the invincible T-34 tanks rolled down the twin roads that converged on Uijongbu. They smashed through every barrier, while their rifleman comrades drove the shattered remnants of the ROK units into the hills.

By the time the United Nations Security Council began assembling at Lake Success, New York, the straight road south from Uijongbu to Seoul lay open to the enemy.

The United Nations, of course, is an international agency founded to keep peace among men. Under the U.N. Charter, chief responsibility for this is assigned to the Security Council. The Council is made up of eleven members, five of whom have permanent seats. The other six seats are filled, in turn, by all the other nations. The five permanent members are the

A view of Seoul, showing the contrast between ancient and modern buildings.

Soviet Union, Great Britain, France, Nationalist China, and the United States. Any of these five members can, by a veto, cancel any action of the Council. Thus the Soviet Union could certainly have vetoed the United States proposal for a cease-fire in Korea. But she did not. Why?

In January of 1950, shortly after Communist China had defeated Nationalist China, the Russians demanded that Nationalist China's place as a permanent member of the Council be given to Red China. They announced that until this was done they would stay away from all Security Council sessions. So on the momentous afternoon of June 25, 1950, the Security Council convened with the Russian chair empty. And the veto that could have prevented a call for a cease-fire in Korea was never used.

The cease-fire order voted by the U.N. Security Council went out immediately, together with an order to the North Korean forces to withdraw above the 38th Parallel. These actions of the Security Council were authorized by a vote of 9–0. Communist Yugoslavia alone abstained from voting.

Meanwhile, the United States moved swiftly. On the evening of June 25th, President Truman gathered his advisors and defense chiefs around him. As a result of this conference, an order went out to General Douglas MacArthur, Supreme Commander of Allied powers in Japan, Commander in Chief of U.S. Forces, Far East, and Commanding General, U.S. Army, Far East. The order said:

> Assist in evacuating United States dependents and noncombatants. MacArthur authorized to take action by Air and Navy to prevent the Inchon-Seoul-Kimpo area from falling into unfriendly hands.

President Truman also instructed the U.S. Seventh Fleet to sail north from the Philippines to the strait separating the Communist Chinese mainland from the Nationalist Chinese stronghold on Formosa. He did this because he wanted to keep the war from spreading.

America was rushing swiftly to the side of embattled South Korea. But in the Seoul area which General MacArthur had been ordered to protect, it was already too late.

President Truman (right) and Attorney General J. Howard McGrath walk to a top-level conference on the Korean crisis.

The North Koreans not only failed to obey the United Nations order to withdraw but they actually redoubled their blows upon Seoul. By the morning of June 27—the third day of invasion—the rumbling of North Korean artillery could be heard in the capital, and the streets were beginning to fill with crowds of terrified refugees rushing for the safety of the south bank of the broad Han River. All that these unhappy people owned hung from wooden A-frames strapped to their backs, or was piled high in little vehicles drawn by oxen. Soon the four bridges over the Han—consisting of three railway spans and one three-lane highway crossing—were crowded with white-robed Koreans. And along with them went military vehicles moving south at a bumper-to-bumper rate

All day long this exodus grew in numbers, spurred by the approaching rumble of enemy artillery. All day long, too the North Koreans punched closer to Seoul. Their tanks were everywhere invincible, even on that stubborn eastern sector, which had at last caved in. Once a gallant South Korean colonel struck at the enemy armor with explosives, destroying four tanks; but otherwise the ROK retreat was complete.

By midnight, United States Ambassador Muccio

A Korean refugee plods along with all his possessions hanging from the wooden A-frame strapped to his back.

had abandoned Seoul for Suwon, fifteen miles south, and the government of President Rhee was in full flight for Taegu still farther below the capital. By that time, also, the Han River bridges were swarming with humanity. In the midst of this chaotic flight, the ROK deputy chief of staff informed his American advisor, Major George Sedberry, that he was going to blow up the bridges.

Thunderstruck, Sedberry telephoned his superior, Lieutenant Colonel Walter Greenwood. Aware that the bulk of the ROK army was still north of the bridges, Greenwood rushed to ROK headquarters to get the order changed. There was a long argument while the demolition deadline of 1:30 A.M. drew ever closer. Finally, the ROK deputy chief of staff ordered one of his officers, Major General Chang Chang Kuk, to drive to the river to countermand the orders of the engineers already in position south of the bridges.

General Chang jumped into his jeep, and plunged into the mass of stalled traffic that blocked all the approaches to the highway bridge. Minutes turned into quarter-hours, and then into agonizing half-hours, until at last Chang could see the police telephone booth on the north side of the river.

Then he saw the night sky turn orange and felt the lash of the terrible explosions that dropped the south end of the Han bridges into the water. With them went uncounted thousands of refugees. The last escape route for the shattered army of the Republic of Korea was sealed off.

South Korean soldiers had to abandon all their trucks and other vehicles, as well as their heavy weapons. Slowly they drifted eastward through the hills to work their way down the east coast, or to cross the river at night by raft or by swimming. They were demoralized and disorganized. By the end of June the ROK army of 98,000 men was down to 22,000. Although this figure would eventually rise again to 54,000, after all the stragglers had reported in, the fact remained that 44,000 men had been lost, as well as 30 per cent of the army's small arms.

The premature blowing of the Han River bridges was nothing less than a military calamity.

A ROK soldier (left) reports to his superior officer.

The day after, June 28th, the tanks and trucks of North Korea clattered into Seoul in triumph, and the communist radio station in the capital at Pyongyang jubilantly predicted that the rest of South Korea would fall before the United States or any other country could interfere.

The war in Korea was now a dramatic race against time.

Enter the United Nations

4

During those first four days of battle, ending in the fall of Seoul, decisions were made in the United States and the United Nations which changed the course of world history.

In Washington on June 26th another dramatic meeting produced the decisions which put America into the Korean War on the side of the ROKs. General MacArthur was ordered to use United States air and naval forces against all North Korean troops south of the 38th Parallel.

Partial view of the conference table during the Security Council meeting to discuss the Korean question. American Ambassador Warren Austin is at the extreme right; the U.S.S.R. seat is empty.

American ground troops were not committed because it was hoped that American air and sea power would be enough to halt the invaders.

The next day the U.N. Security Council met once more, the Russians again being absent, and passed the historic resolution which ranged the United Nations against the communist invaders. This momentous document declared:

> Having noted from the report of the United Nations Commission for Korea that the authorities in North Korea have neither ceased hostilities nor withdrawn their armed forces to the 38th Parallel and that urgent military measures are required to restore international peace and security, and
>
> Having noted the appeal from the Republic of Korea to the United Nations for immediate and effective steps to secure peace and security,
>
> [The Security Council] recommends that the Members of the United Nations furnish such assistance to the Republic of Korea as may be necessary to repel the armed attack and to restore international peace and security in the area.

For the first time a world organization of states had taken up arms to oppose aggression and keep the peace. Eleven days later another great milestone was passed when the Council authorized a unified United Nations Command for Korea and asked the United States to appoint its commander. Soviet Russia was again absent. She did not return to the Council until August, and then she solemnly pronounced that everything done in her absence was "illegal."

But the communist world's great blunder had been made. By staying away from the Council, Russia had allowed the United Nations to rush to the side of South Korea. All member nations were asked to contribute troops, arms, money, supplies, or medical aid to the great cause. Russia, of course, ignored this request, as did all other communist countries. But eventually fifty-three members of the world organization made some sort of contribution.

One of the first to offer assistance was Great Britain. On the fourth day of battle, the very day of the first great U.N. resolution, Admiral C. Turner Joy, Commander of U.S. Naval Forces, Far East, received this message from Admiral Sir Patrick Brind, Commander in Chief of the British Far Eastern Station at Hong Kong:

> I shall be very glad to know of any operation in which my ships could help. Present dispositions are Task Group 96.8 in South Japan under Rear Admiral Andrewes consisting of *Triumph, Belfast, Jamaica,* two destroyers and three frigates. . . .

Australia and New Zealand quickly made similar offers, followed by Canada. France, already bleeding under communist attacks in Indochina, sent a battalion led by Lieutenant Colonel Ralph

Above: Two members of the Ethiopian battalion in Korea ready their mortar for action. Below: A Belgian battalion prepares to sail for the Far East.

KAM INA

Monclar, a veteran of the Foreign Legion who gave up his three-star rank of *Général de Corps D'Armée* to fight in Korea. Turkey furnished a brigade, and five thousand riflemen came from the Philippines. Thailand provided a ship and a regiment, while Colombia and the Netherlands sent a battalion and a small warship apiece. A fighter squadron arrived from South Africa, and Belgium and Ethiopia each volunteered a battalion. Little Luxembourg dispatched a company of soldiers, and Greece placed an infantry battalion and an air transport squadron in the battle. From nations with a policy of neutrality there came missions of mercy: hospital units from Sweden, Norway, and Italy; a hospital ship from Denmark, and a field ambulance from India.

In time, the soldiers of sixteen nations rallied for actual fighting beneath the blue-and-white banner of the United Nations. They did not all come at once and their presence tended to complicate the United Nations Command which Douglas MacArthur was named to lead. There were so many differences in food, dress, language, and custom. But their coming was one of the noble movements of history and, much as they differed, these men had a common love of a nation's right to be free.

For the first time in history, men were putting aside their differences to fight together for someone else's freedom. And the first soldiers to do this were Americans.

Enter the Americans

5

President Truman had not wanted to send American ground forces into Korea. There were many reasons for this besides his hope that United States air and sea power could halt the invaders. For one thing, American occupation troops were needed in Japan to defend that country against a possible attack by a communist country. Moreover, it was always possible that Premier Stalin might have started a war in Asia as a trap. This is an old military trick—to strike in one place in order to draw your enemy's forces away from the place where you really want to strike. In this case Truman feared that the Communists' true objective might be Europe, with all its factories and scientists and skilled workers. Stalin might want to get America and her allies bogged down in Asia so that he could gobble up more of Europe.

Finally, the President was also afraid that, if American divisions went into Korea, Stalin would send in Russian divisions to oppose them. And this could touch off World War III.

But then Truman received a very gloomy report from General Douglas MacArthur, who had flown to Korea from Tokyo and made a bold scouting trip right up to the Han River. What General MacArthur saw convinced him that only immediate use of American ground troops could save South Korea from being overrun by the North Koreans.

Thus, on June 30th, President Truman authorized the use of ground forces. American troops were to be rushed from Japan to hold the onrushing Communists at bay until more men and guns arrived, making it possible for the United Nations Command to mount its own counterattack.

This kind of "delaying action" is among the most difficult of military maneuvers. Fortunately, the man chosen to carry it out was one of the best officers in the American army. Tall, lean as a whiplash, with crew-cut sandy hair, Major General William Dean was a man of great will power and high personal courage. He had led the 44th Infantry Division in World War II and had at one time been military governor of South Korea. At the moment, he commanded the U.S. 24th Infantry Division in Japan.

General Dean moved swiftly. He ordered Lieutenant Colonel Charles ("Brad") Smith to assemble all available men from his 1st Battalion, 21st Infantry Regiment, and to speed to Itazuke Airfield. Colonel Smith literally jumped from his bed after getting the telephoned order and collected his men—a bare 406 of them. In a dismal night rain these mystified men and officers grabbed their weapons, clambered into trucks and went careening off to Itazuke. There General

Major General William F. Dean makes his inaugural address as the new military governor of Korea.

Dean met Colonel Smith and gave him further instructions:

"When you get to Pusan, head for Taejon. We want to stop the North Koreans as far from Pusan as we can. Block the main road as far north as possible. . . . Sorry I can't give you more information. That's all I've got. Good luck to you, and God bless you and your men."

Colonel Smith saluted and then his men filed aboard the transports waiting in the drizzle. One by one, the squat gray shapes lumbered onto the runway to rise roaring into the mists. "Task Force Smith," as this unit was to be known, was on its way.

The port of Pusan, to which tiny Task Force Smith was winging, was the finest in South Korea. It was at the extreme southern tip of the peninsula, and there General MacArthur had decided to build his forces for the eventual counterstrike against the Reds. He had already decided that all the units sent to Korea by United Nations countries would be placed in the U.S. Eighth Army. The Eighth Army would act for the United Nations Command in the field. This, of course, seemed only fair, for the United States was contributing ten times as much in men and munitions as all the other volunteering nations combined. South Korea herself was contributing the most troops, but these ROK divisions would also be under control of the Eighth Army.

Pusan was important, and the Communists knew it as well as MacArthur. That was why they had sent their finest divisions, the 3rd and 4th, clattering out of Seoul on a wild race for Pusan. If they could get there before the United Nations Command built up its forces, they could close off all Korea to the United Nations.

By the time Task Force Smith was airborne, the crack North Korean 3rd and 4th divisions had already made a fighting crossing of the Han River. And they had battled into Seoul's important industrial suburb of Yongdongpo. Their next objective was Suwon Airfield, from which most of the American civilians in Korea had already been evacuated. From Suwon, the Reds would then dash down the road to Pusan and the war

South Koreans welcome United States infantrymen arriving at Taejon.

in Korea would be over.

This was the situation on July 1st, when the men of Task Force Smith landed at Pusan Airfield and were driven north along flag-bedecked streets lined with thousands of cheering, wildly happy South Koreans. Trains took them still farther north until, by July 5th, they had come to a pair of hills above Osan on the Seoul-Pusan road.

American foot soldiers leave the railroad station en route to the front.

By that time the North Korean army had shattered all remaining South Korean resistance on the western side of the peninsula. Over on the eastern coast, heavy rains and rock slides and the shells of United States Navy bombardment forces had slowed down the communist advance. So it was now-or-never on the west coast as the enemy 4th Division rolled out of Suwon.

Colonel Smith chose his position at Osan well. There were now 540 Americans in his command, after the arrival of 134 artillerymen with five 105-millimeter howitzers. Unfortunately, only one of these precious guns was supplied with antitank shells capable of piercing a Russian T-34, and there were only six of these shells. The rest of the ammunition was ordinary high explosive. So Colonel Smith put most of his hope in the lone gun supplied with the six antitank shells.

First he fortified hills on either side of the road. Soldiers with rifles, machine guns, mortars, bazookas, and 75-millimeter recoilless rifles went into place on both heights. Behind the left or western hill, Colonel Smith put his antitank gun so that it could shoot at any tanks which successfully ran the gantlet between the hills. Still farther behind this gun, also on the left, went the other four howitzers provided with high-explosive shells.

All was in readiness when the gray rain-swept daylight of July 5th dawned at Osan. American soldiers crouching in their ponchos reflected on the fortunes of war that had shifted them, in five days, from the warmth and gaiety of Japan to the miserable rain and mud of the Korean monsoon. The smell of human dung, wafted up from the surrounding pale green of the rice paddies, made it difficult to eat their cold C-rations.

Then—eight great beetle shapes rolled slowly out of the rain mists below Suwon. The Americans gasped. The squat shapes were tanks, the spearhead of thirty-three armored T-34s leading approximately 10,000 North Korean soldiers down the road.

Quickly Task Force Smith's forward observer called for artillery strikes. At exactly 8:16 A.M. the first American artillery shell of the war howled toward the enemy. The observer noted its impact and adjusted his range. Soon the shells were exploding among the tanks. Some began to make direct hits, but they merely sparked harmlessly off the monsters' thick skins.

The tanks came on.

When they had rolled to within 700 yards of the American position, Colonel Smith ordered his 75-millimeter recoilless rifle teams to open up. They did, sometimes scoring direct hits, but still the tanks came on. Soon the T-34s were within range of the 2.36-inch rocket launchers or bazookas. When the tanks were abreast of the bazookas, Lieutenant Ollie Connor fired at one of them from a distance of only fifteen yards. His bazooka flamed with the rocket's backlash, but the tank waddled past unscathed. Lieutenant Connor's section fired twenty-two rockets from a roadside ditch, but they couldn't stop the T-34s.

Now all thirty-three of the enemy tanks were in view, following the spearhead in groups of four. At last two of the eight spearhead tanks shot the pass between Smith's hills, emerging in full view of the American antitank howitzer.

Wham! Ba-loom!

Six antitank shells shrieked forth, and the two tanks lurched and came to a halt. They pulled off the road, where one of them burst into flame. As its turret flipped open, two North Korean soldiers popped out, holding their hands high. Then a third soldier jumped up, firing a burp gun straight into an American machine-gun position. He killed a soldier—the first American to die in the Korean conflict—and was killed in turn by other Americans. At the same time, the rest of the Red tanks began to roll through the pass.

They came clanking along at full throttle, hatches buttoned down, firing blindly, sometimes even to the east side of the road where there were no guns. They got through the American artillery with little difficulty. Ordinary high-explosive shells could not pierce their armor, although two T-34s were hit in the treads, disabled, and later destroyed.

T-34 tank knocked out by U.N. troops.

The others raced down on the defenseless city of Osan, while behind them North Korean infantrymen came to grips with Smith's soldiers.

An hour after the enemy tanks had broken through the American position, Colonel Smith saw trucks full of enemy soldiers coming along the road from Suwon. Leading them were three more tanks, which formed the tail of the armored column. Smith calmly allowed the column to come on. In another hour the leading trucks were within a range of 1,000 yards.

"Fire!" Smith cried.

The Americans opened up with everything they had. Rifles cracked, machine guns hammered, 75-millimeter guns boomed, and mortars whuffled overhead. Enemy trucks began bursting into flame and the bodies of their passengers flew through the air.

It was the fiercest blow struck by Task Force Smith, but it did not break the North Koreans. With swift precision, the trucks pulled off the road. The soldiers hid themselves in ditches, and the three T-34s rolled forward to rake Smith's

Lieutenant Colonel Charles ("Brad") Smith

hill positions with cannon and machine-gun fire. Then the North Korean soldiers attacked.

One big force went wide around Smith's right-hand hill, and another seized a height above the left-hand hill to send fire plunging down into it. Smith had to call his left-side force over to his own position on the right. But then the North Koreans moved to surround him, and Colonel Smith gave the order to pull back.

As the Americans withdrew, the North Koreans, highly expert in automatic weapons, cut loose with a withering, grass-cutting machine-gun fire. It broke up Smith's unit, and it drew the most blood of the Osan fighting. Before the enemy gunners had eased up on their triggers, Task Force Smith ceased to exist as a fighting unit.

Men broke for the hills or waded through the stinking rice paddies. Colonel Smith himself moved back to collect his artillery, finally organizing a truck column that sped south for Osan. But finding the town in enemy hands, he turned hastily around until he found a safe road east to Ansong.

All along his retreating journey Smith picked up stragglers from his unit. Many more of them drifted south through the hills. So it was many days until the full fate of Task Force Smith was known. Of 540 men, approximately 150 were killed, wounded, or reported missing (probably captured). The epitaph for Task Force Smith was written by a young North Korean soldier who noted in his diary that night:

> We met vehicles and American POWs. We also saw some American dead. We found four of our destroyed tanks. Near Osan there was a great battle.

General Dean's Last Stand

6

Major General William Dean was deeply disappointed by the defeat of Task Force Smith. The General had flown to Korea—risking his life in a wild, mountain-dodging flight in a small plane. Since his arrival he had been busy trying to get more units of his division into action, while raising the drooping fighting spirit of the west-coast ROKs.

He had little luck with the South Koreans, who were so disorganized that he could not depend on them. But he was able to bring the 34th Regiment of his 24th Division into Korea. He had hoped to send the 34th up to join Task Force Smith in the delaying action, but there had been no such delay. So General Dean had to be satisfied with putting two battalions of the 34th into a blocking position at the towns of Pyongtaek and Ansong. The Pyongtaek-Ansong line was about ten miles south of Osan.

Here, too, the Americans could not hold, for once again they were outnumbered and outgunned. It seemed that nothing could halt those terrible T-34s. Worse, some of the American troops withdrew even before the battle at Pyongtaek-Ansong began.

General Dean was enraged when he heard of it, and he drove north to halt this unauthorized retreat. But when the General found the men, it was nearly nightfall. He dared not risk an ambush at night, so he allowed them to stay where they were, at a place called Chonan, fifteen miles south of Pyongtaek. The Americans now stood about 60 miles south of Seoul and 110 miles northwest of vital Pusan.

A Marine Corsair fighter plane takes off from the carrier USS Bataan.

On July 8th Chonan also fell, but the valor of its defenders had risen under the gallant leadership of Colonel Robert Martin, who lost his life in the battle. He had seized a light bazooka to duel with an enemy tank, and a shell from an 85-millimeter struck him.

The North Koreans were now beginning to slow down. And they could no longer move in daylight, for American air power was asserting itself. Mustangs and Shooting Stars of the U.S. Fifth Air Force, as well as Marine and Navy fighters from American aircraft carriers, had begun to attack the North Korean columns. Enemy tank losses were mounting.

On July 8th, the day that Chonan fell, General Dean put in an urgent call for some of the new 3.5-inch bazookas. These would be capable of destroying the T-34s. In his report to General MacArthur he said:

"I am convinced that the North Korean army, the North Korean soldier, and his status of training and quality of equipment have been underestimated."

MacArthur lost no time in relaying this report to the defense chiefs in Washington, declaring:

"I strongly urge that in addition to those forces already requisitioned, an army of at least four divisions . . . be dispatched to this area without delay and by every means of transportation available.

"The situation has developed into a major operation."

That message electrified officials in Washington. General Dean's badly needed bazookas were rushed aboard airplanes in California, and more units were notified to stand by for movement to the battle zone. Meanwhile, the 1st Provisional Marine Brigade was already taking ship for Korea from California, and the 1st Cavalry Division was scheduled to move into action from Japan.

But even with these reinforcements and supplies en route, it was still touch-and-go along the western road from Seoul to Pusan. The enemy's central advance had been slowed down by mountains, and his eastern progress had been delayed by a narrow coastal road defended by ROKs with the support of American air and sea power. But the Seoul-Pusan road remained a critical sector. And now General Dean had received two battalions of another regiment—the 21st—to help hold it. This outfit went into line below Chonan, fighting savagely under Colonel Richard Stephens.

On July 10th, American light tanks entered the battle with the battalions from the 21st Regiment, but they were no match for the bigger T-34s. On that same day, Colonel Stephens' regiment fell back to a place called Chochiwon.

"Hold in your position and fight . . . !" General Dean ordered Colonel Stephens.

The 21st did fight hard, but still could not hold against an enemy who had now become desperate to batter down all resistance. But even though the regiment had to withdraw, its men had slowed down the North Korean timetable by two days. During that time, General Dean's last regiment—the 19th—had come to the rescue, and there were elements of another division, the U.S. 25th Infantry, arriving in Korea. The big bombers of the U.S. Far East Air Force were hammering the enemy columns in the central mountains, while the Marine Brigade was racing at flank speed for Pusan. The 1st Cavalry was being rushed to a little fishing harbor on the east coast.

But these reinforcements would not arrive for a few more days. Until they did, General Dean and the men of his 24th Division had to delay the enemy more. They *had* to hang on. So Dean sent the battered 21st Regiment into reserve and put the 19th and the 34th regiments into position at a bend of the Kum River. This river was like a moat around the important communications center at Taejon, a city almost

An American soldier in a foxhole faces the no man's land along the shallow Kum River.

exactly halfway between Seoul and Pusan. Dean hoped to hold at the Kum until a good defensive line could be built up at Taejon.

But the North Koreans struck with massed fury and got around the American regiments. Although the steadily dwindling ranks of the enemy's 3rd and 4th divisions were again reduced, and more tanks and trucks lost, they kept coming. Premier Kim Il Sung was boasting that the Americans would be hurled into the sea long before their reinforcements could arrive.

To aid their advance, the North Korean commanders adopted the cruel practice of "recruiting" young South Korean civilians at gunpoint, or of launching "refugee attacks." They gathered hundreds of the South Korean refugees who were streaming south in great droves. Herding them together in a tight mass—woman and children first—the North Korean troops drove the helpless refugees at bayonet point into an American battle position. Mingling with the mob were North Korean soldiers in civilian dress—grenades and burp guns hidden beneath flowing white robes. Behind the masses of hapless refugees were the North Korean assault units themselves.

Rain fell for three or four days at a time—making everything soft and squashy to the touch, rotting a man's clothes and rusting his rifle. These rains were followed by a moist and steaming heat in which men already soaked by rain continued to drip in their own sweat. Mud was

Above: By placing rocks in rain-soaked mud, South Korean workers provide a solid road base for the truckload of 1st Cavalry troops waiting in the background. Below: Heavy rains hamper the withdrawal of ROK troops.

everywhere, clutching at a soldier's feet, putting an agonizing strain on calf muscles grown soft in the garrison duty of Japan. And when units had to move through rice paddies, the ordeal of fighting a delaying action was made miserably complete. Here was human filth and a constant sickening reek, along with flies, fleas, and other pests.

Yet these Americans fought on, falling back to fight again and then fall back once more. They were trading space for time, and buying it in blood and misery—until they made their last stand at Taejon.

General Dean had not planned a last-ditch fight in that vital little city. He had hoped to hold his position just a day, while preparing a stronger position at Yongdong twenty-eight miles to the east. But when he was ordered to hold fast for at least two days, he had no choice. The United States Navy had sailed on the skirts of a typhoon to put a regiment of the 1st Cavalry Division ashore on the east coast. Time was required until these soldiers could be rushed by train to Yongdong.

General Dean prepared his defenses, issuing his men the new big bazookas which had been flown into Korea. With these, Dean hoped to stop the T-34s. He believed that any enemy tank moving through a city guarded by hidden U.N. soldiers firing such weapons would be, as he put it, "a dead duck." On July 19th, the two-pronged North Korean assault on Taejon began.

One enemy column struck from the west and another attacked from the northwest behind the fiercest artillery barrage of the war. Gradually another smaller column detached itself from the western prong. It began to swing southeast in an effort to come up on Taejon through the back door. General Dean had left this approach open when he pulled his troops up from the south.

The gallant general was everywhere, rallying his men, seeking to stem the communist tide. In the west he led two tanks to a bridge to hold the position there, returning to the city to direct the entire battle. But the Reds were throwing in fresh reserves and hammering the weary Americans with artillery. That night they launched a fresh assault, and at three o'clock in the morning of the 20th their tanks burst through the northwestern position and sped down on Taejon. At daylight, another tank column slipped up through the wide-open back door and rolled into the city. Snipers in civilian clothes rode the tanks, dropping off to dart into empty buildings. From concealed hideouts they began a terrible harrying of the retreating Americans.

By then Taejon was on fire. Buildings that had been set blazing by exploding shells—especially the white phosphorus of the mortars—set adjoining structures alight. Soon the city was a roaring, crackling holocaust. In this red oven, the Americans and North Koreans carried on a deadly rifle fight. General Dean, aware now that Taejon was lost, boldly roved the streets with a bazooka. Finally, from the window of a burning building, he got a tank in his sights and could make his famous report: "Today I got me a tank."

General Dean had no choice but to organize an orderly withdrawal. He formed truck columns and set them speeding toward the last escape route east. He entered one of the last vehicles himself and roared away. But his driver took a wrong turning, even as the Communists cut that last escape route east, and General Dean found himself speeding south straight for enemy positions. Meanwhile, on the poplar-lined eastern road held by the Communists, the retreating American soldiers found themselves moving along an avenue of death.

So ended the fifteen-day ordeal of the 24th Infantry Division. It had begun when Task Force Smith went up the road to Osan, and it ended in the fiery stand at Taejon. Two days later this battered division turned its positions over to the 1st Cavalry Division and went into reserve. And General Dean?

The night he left Taejon he fell down a slope while going after water for some wounded men. He was knocked unconscious. When he awoke, his shoulder throbbed with pain. It was broken. The General wandered through the hills for thirty-six days, trying to get back to his men. His weight fell from 190 pounds to 130, and finally he was betrayed to the enemy by two

South Korean civilians who pretended to be his friends. For the rest of the war, General Dean was a prisoner of the North Koreans, as bold and unbreakable in captivity as in battle. Upon his release, he was astonished to find that a grateful nation had awarded him its highest decoration, the Medal of Honor.

General Dean had not known that he and his men had done what was asked of them: they had delayed the enemy rush. Even as he awoke in pain on that July 21st, the 1st Cavalry was in line at Yongdong and the crisis had passed.

The great days of the Pusan Perimeter were at hand.

Bulldog Walker at Pusan

7

Lieutenant General Walton Walker's nickname was "Johnny." But many of the war correspondents in Korea had begun to call him "Bulldog." That was the way General Walker was built—short, powerful, with determined outthrust jaw. And that was the way he fought.

In World War I, Walker led a machine-gun company and won a battlefield promotion. During the early 1930s, he commanded the 15th Infantry in China, and then went on to become famous in World War II as an armored corps commander for the dashing General George S. Patton. In 1948, General Walker came to Japan to take over the Eighth Army; and on July 6, 1950, General MacArthur told him that the Eighth would control the United Nations Command in action. Luckily for the U.N. cause, Bulldog Walker's tenacious, hang-on-at-all-costs fighting spirit was exactly what was needed to defend the Pusan Perimeter.

Such a perimeter is actually a line of defense. In American pioneer days the circle formed by covered wagons as a protection against Indian attacks was a kind of defensive perimeter. At Pusan the defensive perimeter was a rectangle approximately eighty miles long by sixty miles wide. On two sides the line was protected by men and arms; on the other two it was bounded by water. There were two vital places inside this perimeter: Pusan, the port into which men and supplies could come; and Taegu, the nerve center where President Syngman Rhee had his government and General Walker maintained his headquarters. Taegu was connected to Pusan by

PUSAN PERIMETER DEFENSE:

August, 1950

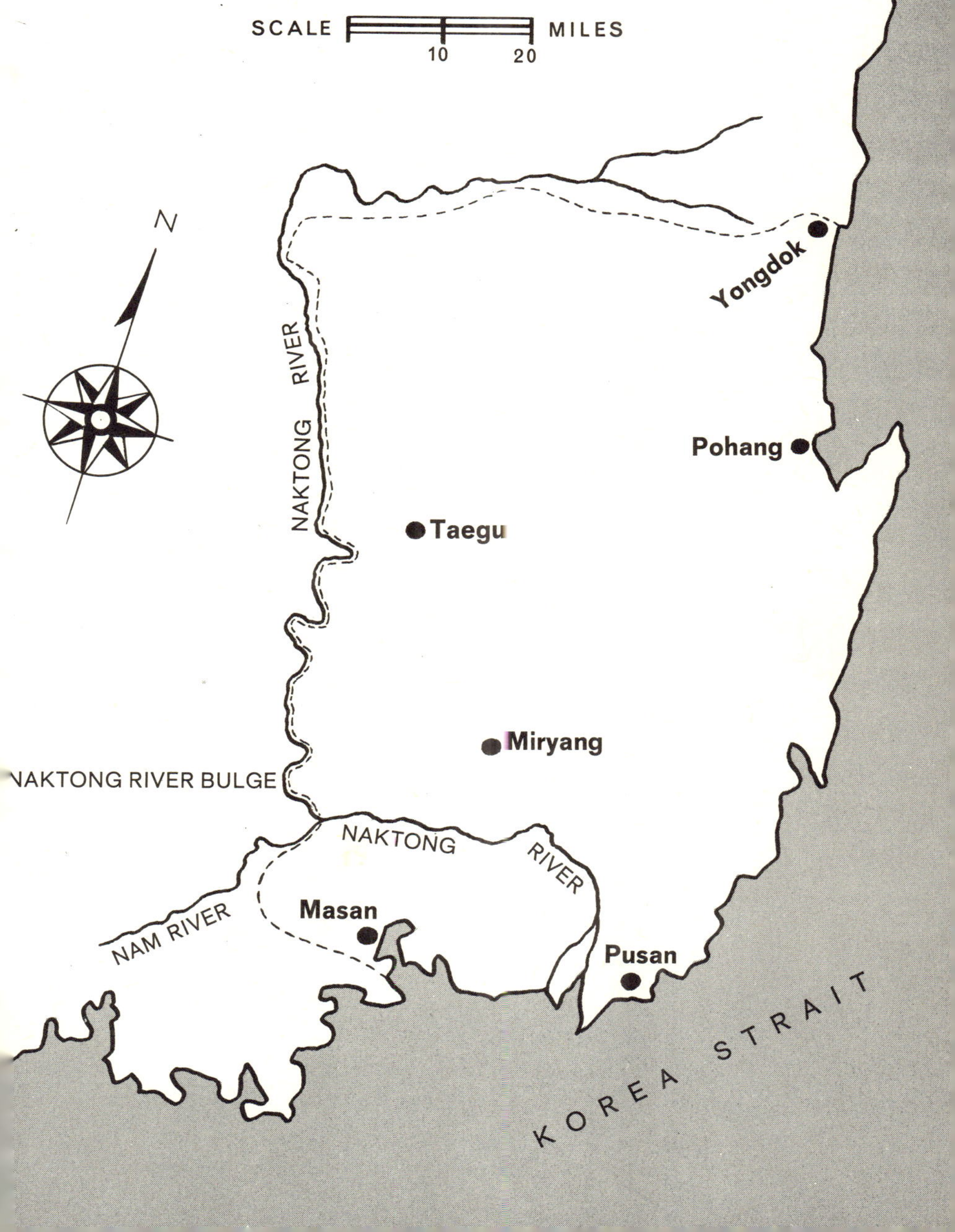

a straight road running about fifty miles to the south.

Although the North Korean armies headed down all the roads to Pusan, hoping to overwhelm the U.N. forces by sheer numbers, the road they wanted most was the Taegu-Pusan road. They wanted either to capture Taegu itself, or to cut the road between that city and Pusan. Then Rhee's government and Walker's headquarters would be cut off.

For this reason approximately a dozen North Korean divisions struck at Taegu from the north, and at the Taegu-Pusan road from west and east (or left and right). It was General Walker's job to fend them off. He moved his units from place to place, quelling the attacks as they broke out, always tending to the biggest battles first. Sometimes he would let the smaller actions rage on—hoping to stop them eventually with artillery fire or aerial bombing. Sometimes, as on the east coast, the mighty guns of United States warships would hold the Communists at bay.

It was a risky business, and it might never have succeeded if General Walker hadn't had the

Lieutenant General Walton Walker

help of units such as the 27th Infantry (Wolfhound) Regiment. The Wolfhounds were part of the U.S. 25th Infantry Division, which had joined the 1st Cavalry and 24th in Korea. Walker used them unsparingly, bolstering a breaking line here, rushing to fill a gap there with a fierce counterattack.

The ROKs, meanwhile, had reorganized their army, though they still possessed only small arms. Also, the big Pershing tanks, easily the equal of the T-34s, were beginning to come into Korea. Their arrival helped General Walker, although moving a tank over a muddy road clogged with refugees was sometimes next to impossible.

On August 2nd, the 1st Marine Brigade arrived, and Walker had a second seasoned outfit to help him plug the holes in his weakened perimeter defenses. Almost all of the officers and about seventy per cent of the men in the Marine Brigade had been in battle against Japan during World War II. In addition to the Marine Brigade, there was an experienced group of fighter pilots —men of the 1st Marine Air Wing—flying big gull-winged Corsairs off two United States Navy carriers. Whenever the marines ran into stubborn opposition, they would radio for the Corsairs. With bombs, rockets, and flaming wing guns, the fighter pilots would attack the enemy position until it was wiped out and the Marine riflemen could move on.

Fighting this way, the Marine Brigade, commanded by Brigadier General Edward Craig, gave Walker his first real victory of the Pusan fighting. This was a counterattack in the west which drove the enemy back a distance of twenty-six miles. But once the counterattack had been successfully carried out, the marines were hastily ordered back within the perimeter.

The Communist 4th Division had crossed the Naktong River on the northwest and was threatening to take Miryang, midway on the vital Taegu-Pusan road. If they did, it could be disaster. So Walker pulled the marines back and ordered them to oust the enemy from this Naktong River Bulge. Here is what a British army officer wrote of that crisis:

> The situation is critical and Miryang may be lost.

> The enemy have driven a division-sized salient across the Naktong. More will cross the river tonight. If Miryang is lost Taegu becomes untenable and we will be faced with a withdrawal from Korea. I am heartened that the Marine Brigade will move against the Naktong salient tomorrow. They are faced with impossible odds, and I have no valid reason to substantiate it, but I have a feeling they will halt the enemy.
>
> I realize my expression of hope is unsound, but these Marines have the swagger, confidence and hardness that must have been in Stonewall Jackson's Army of the Shenandoah. They remind me of the Coldstreams at Dunkerque. Upon this thin line of reasoning, I cling to the hope of victory.

The Brigade's rifle regiment—the famous Fifth Marines—assaulted the Bulge at a place called No-Name Ridge on August 17th. Twice they attacked, and twice they were repulsed. But by nightfall they had again battled up to the summit of two of No-Name's hills.

Next day they renewed the attack, only to be halted by a nest of enemy machine guns. The

Above: A U.N. scouting party beside the Naktong River watches enemy movements near a bridge demolished by U.S. Army engineers. Below: American troops seize a strategic hilltop within the Pusan Perimeter.

position was marked with a smoke rocket, and a Corsair flown by Captain John Kelley dived down to drop a 500-pound bomb squarely athwart it. The explosion stunned the marines for a moment. Then, rising with a yell, they swept forward in the final thrust that drove the North Koreans back and into the Naktong.

"The enemy was killed in such numbers," said the log of the carrier *Sicily,* "that the river was definitely discolored with blood."

Though the greatest threat had been beaten back, there were other critical moments ahead for Bulldog Walker. The North Korean army was about to launch its Great Naktong Offensive. This drive, ordered by the Red supreme commander in Pyongyang, was conducted by General Kim Chaik. Kim hurled 98,000 men against the U.N. forces during late August and early September.

But by then, the U.N. Command had also grown. There were now 180,000 men under Walker's control, including 1,500 soldiers of the newly arrived British Brigade, and 91,500 ROKs.

The South Koreans, not part of the Eighth Army, were still subject to its control under a verbal agreement between President Rhee and General MacArthur.

So Walker now had enough forces to contain the Communists during the wild fighting that raged on both banks of the Naktong River as it flowed west around Taegu, then turned south to the sea. It was a chaotic, constantly shifting struggle. Here the enemy would cross a river; there they would be hurled back. Here a U.N. unit would sit in safety, like an island in a thundering sea of conflict; and there another would be battered repeatedly by wave after wave of enemy soldiers.

Then from the west came the fiercest blow of all. Once again there was a Naktong River Bulge; once again the Taegu-Pusan road was imperiled, this time by 30,000 enemy soldiers. As before, Walker threw the Marine Brigade into the breech. They counterattacked and regained lost ground, after which—with the help of the U.S. 2nd Infantry Division—they broke the enemy threat to pieces.

Thus, gradually, the North Korean attempt to get to Pusan was defeated. And yet the enemy troops continued to hammer vainly at that southern gate to Korea, unaware that General Douglas MacArthur had already ordered that great counterstroke which was to fall behind them and cut them off.

The Glory of MacArthur

8

General of the Army Douglas MacArthur had already established a brilliant reputation in the annals of American warfare.

Born the son of a famous general, Arthur MacArthur, young Douglas was what is called an "Army brat"—a youngster who grows up with the sound of bugles or marching feet forever in his ears.

He went to West Point, made the baseball varsity, and was graduated at the top of his class, having established a scholastic record that still stands. After graduating he went to the Philippines, where a rebel's bullet took his hat off. In 1911, the dashing Captain MacArthur almost won a Medal of Honor for a daring scouting mission into Mexico during the Vera Cruz Expedition. In World War I he led the famous Rainbow Division, the youngest general to hold such command. Then he was, successively, the youngest man to be superintendent of West Point and the youngest Army Chief of Staff in history. That would seem career enough for any man, yet Douglas MacArthur went on to reorganize the Philippine Army.

After the Japanese strike at Pearl Harbor, MacArthur was recalled to duty in the United States Army and given command of the Southwest Pacific. His masterly campaigns against the Japanese ended in his receiving the Japanese surrender aboard the battleship *Missouri,* after which he became the Supreme Allied Commander in Japan. Then came the crisis in Korea and his appointment as U.N. Supreme Commander. With this there also came the opportunity to cap his career

General Douglas MacArthur, commander in chief of U.N. forces in Korea.

with its most glorious achievement.

During the first disastrous week of fighting, General MacArthur had flown to Korea for a first-hand survey of the battlefield. There, on a hill near the Han River, he had watched while the retreat from Seoul washed around him. And it was then that he first thought of landing units deep in the enemy's rear to cut off the North Koreans from their supplies while crushing them to bits between two forces. To do this he would need to land a force at Inchon, the west-coast city which served as a seaport for Seoul. So he asked the defense chiefs in Washington for the 1st Marine Division. This unit was ordered to get to Korea as soon as it could, and the 7th Infantry Division, another crack landing outfit, was also alerted to move.

In the meantime experienced Navy and Marine officers had been pointing out the great difficulties involved in MacArthur's plans for a landing at Inchon. The tides there are the second highest in the world. That is, they rise and fall an average of twenty-nine feet a day, sometimes as much as thirty-six feet in a single day.

And the tides move so fast that a boat can be stranded in ten minutes. Also, there are only a few days every month when the tides are at the maximum height, allowing enough time to get troops and supplies ashore. General MacArthur had only three possible landing dates, September 15th, October 11th, and November 3rd.

Among other objections to Inchon was the fact that Flying Fish Channel, the entrance to the harbor, is very narrow. Since ships would not be able to turn around in it, they would be sitting ducks for enemy coastal guns. The seawall was also an obstacle. Marines clambering up it in assault waves would be exposed to enemy fire. Worse, they would have only an hour or so of daylight in which to fight their way into Inchon. The high tide would not occur until 5:30 P.M., and sunset was due at 6:43 P.M. That would not give much time to seize a big unknown city of 250,000 people and then prepare for enemy counterattacks.

Finally, there was the problem of whether or not the Chinese Communists would intervene to save the North Korean Communists from destruction. They were already known to be moving troops north, and at least four Chinese armies were based due east of Inchon directly across the Yellow Sea. A U.N. invasion force jammed into a narrow harbor at Inchon might give Red China just the opportunity she wanted, for the Communists in Peiping were now open and abusive enemies of the United States.

All these arguments were raised by General MacArthur's commanders—Army, Navy, and Marine—when he gathered them around him at his Tokyo headquarters in the Dai Ichi Palace. Also present were the Chief of Staff of the United States Army, General J. Lawton ("Lightning Joe") Collins, and Admiral Forrest Sherman, the Chief of Naval Operations. They, too, disliked the Inchon gamble. MacArthur heard them all out, including his amphibious commander, Admiral Arthur Doyle, who said:

"General, I have not been asked nor have I volunteered my opinion about this landing. If I were asked, however, the best I can say is that Inchon is not impossible."

Even such a remark from the man who would

have charge of the landing fleet did not dampen Douglas MacArthur's ardor. Seated at his desk, he began to speak. Jabbing his famous corncob pipe in the air, pausing twice to refill it, his voice rising to a ringing note, sometimes falling to a whisper, the eloquent Douglas MacArthur made his points. He spoke of how General Wolfe had succeeded at Quebec because General Montcalm never thought he would dare climb the cliff below the Plains of Abraham. He said he would succeed for the same reason: the enemy did not dream he would dare the "impossible landing" at Inchon.

"We must strike hard and deep into enemy territory," he said. "Inchon will not fail, and it will save a hundred thousand lives. I realize that it is a five-thousand-to-one gamble, but I'll accept it. I am used to taking those odds." The great commander paused dramatically and his voice sank to a harsh whisper. "We shall land at Inchon, and I shall crush them!"

Thereafter, no one disputed MacArthur. September 15th was set as the invasion date, and the Navy sent a lieutenant, Eugene Clark, to scout the harbor islands. Clark, who was put ashore the night of September 1st, spent two hair-raising weeks organizing a network of spies to spot enemy gun positions and measure the height of Inchon's seawall.

At half-past two in the morning of September 15th, ships carrying assault marines of the 1st Division slipped into Inchon Harbor. It was a dark night, and there were high winds from a typhoon near Japan. One by one the transports followed the bombardment ships leading them in, sailing at intervals 700 yards apart. Suddenly a light came on in the lighthouse at the mouth of Flying Fish Channel. A Marine officer grinned in the dark, and whispered: "All the comforts of home." He did not know it—no one knew it—but the brave Lieutenant Clark who had scouted the harbor islands was sitting wrapped in a blanket atop the lighthouse. He had turned on the light to guide his countrymen into the narrow channel.

Slowly the dark shapes became distinguishable in the murky light of dawn. Then, at 5:45 A.M.,

Sunrise in Inchon Harbor as seen from the USS Mount McKinley.

the heavy naval bombardment began.

Pah-boom, pah-boom, pah-boom!

American destroyers close to shore, American and British cruisers a few miles back, American rocket ships racing in to release missiles like flights of arrows—all were pounding the unfortunate little spit of land known as Wolmi-do or Moontip Island. For Wolmi was the cork in the Inchon bottle. It guarded all the harbor approaches and it sat right between the two landing areas chosen by the Marines. Wolmi's guns, then, could rake the Americans landing to either side of them.

But Wolmi's guns were being knocked out by the U.N. gunners plotting their targets on information supplied by Lieutenant Clark's spies. Then Marine Corsairs dropped from the skies to strafe the beaches, and at 6:27 the 3rd Battalion, 5th Marines, led by Lieutenant Colonel Robert Taplett went roaring inshore at Wolmi.

The little island's 500 defenders were still too dazed to offer much resistance to the "yellowlegs," a nickname the enemy gave to the Marines because of the canvas leggings they wore.

The Americans raced inland. Soon big Pershing tanks—three of them mounting flamethrowers—were also on Wolmi supporting those fast-moving riflemen in mottled green dungarees. Forty-five minutes after the first American touched Wolmi's soil, Lieutenant Colonel Taplett radioed the fleet:

"Wolmi-do secured."

Aboard the flagship *Mount McKinley,* Douglas MacArthur heaved a great sigh of relief. His eyes shone joyfully. His great gamble had not failed. The worst was over, he was sure, and he rose from his chair on deck and went below to compose this message:

"The Navy and the Marines have never shone more brightly than this morning."

Soon there was American artillery mounted on Wolmi-do, ready to support the landings to left and right. The first unit to hit the Inchon seawall was the one on the left, two battalions of the 5th Marines led by big Lieutenant Colonel Raymond Murray, the man who had won the battle of No-Name Ridge. When these men reached the seawall, the top of it was four feet above the prows of their boats. They had to hook on ladders in order to scramble over it. Some of them even threw each other up and over—leapfrogging into battle, and vanishing in the smoke with a yell and the clatter of small-arms fire. But they swept all before them.

On the right was the 1st Marine Regiment

Marines scramble up scaling ladders to storm ashore at Inchon.

commanded by grizzled Colonel Lewis ("Chesty") Puller, the most battle-scarred and decorated Marine in the history of the Corps. His men went in, dynamiting entry points in the seawall. Sometimes a big landing ship rammed right into the wall, knocking a hole in it. Then the ship's bow doors swung open and a bulldozer rumbled out to cover up the enemy slit trenches. And Chesty Puller's men were also irresistible.

By nightfall the spearheads of the 1st Marine Division were in Inchon to stay. They were dug in defending their vital beachhead, grimly awaiting the expected enemy counter blows. But none came.

Next morning the marines moved through Inchon's streets, while ROK marines behind them were mopping up. The following day they wiped out a North Korean force of 200 men in a tank battle that captured Kimpo Airfield for the United Nations. That same day the 7th Infantry Division landed at Inchon unopposed, striking quickly inland to block the roads offering escape routes to the North Korean divisions down at Pusan.

It was a few more days before the North Koreans at Pusan received the stunning news that the United Nations had landed behind them. When that happened, the cocky army that had raced south from Seoul began to fall apart. From September 22nd on, Bulldog Walker's hang-on battle began to change to a breakout and pursuit. One after another the enemy divisions broke contact and headed north, hoping to get across the 38th Parallel before the U.N. forces could slam shut all doors. All the way they were scourged by U.N. airplanes and struck at by the pursuing South Koreans, Americans, and British.

On the east coast the sixteen-inch guns of the U.S. battleship *Missouri* slammed into the retiring North Koreans. After the "Mighty Mo" lifted her fire, the ROK 3rd Division—"the Rambling ROKs"—came racing up the shore road in pursuit of the frantically back-pedaling enemy.

In the center, some of the thirteen North Korean divisions simply disappeared. Many of the men and officers melted into the mountains to turn to guerrilla fighting or out-and-out banditry.

And on the west coast the spectacular speed of the pursuit was dramatized by the dash of Task Force Lynch, an armored column from the 1st Cavalry Division led by Lieutenant Colonel James Lynch. In three days, Task Force Lynch sped 105 miles north from Poun to join up with 7th Division soldiers at Suwon. It had taken the North Korean 2nd Division about a month to travel that same distance during its drive south from Seoul, and this showed how completely the fortunes of war had changed.

Up at Seoul, meanwhile, the most savage battle of the war was developing in that unhappy city's streets. It began on September 25th, when Chesty Puller's 1st Marines smashed into the city's outer defenses. The Americans had to move against street barricades covered by enemy machine guns and antitank cannon. It was blow-for-blow, shot-for-shot fighting of the most deadly kind, and much of it was done at night. But the marines won out, helped in the end by the ROK 17th Division and the 32nd Regiment of the U.S. 7th Division.

On September 29th, General Douglas MacAr-

군 만세!

thur flew into Kimpo Airfield and drove through the blackened, smoking ruins of Seoul to fire-gutted Government House. Standing under a broken skylight in the presence of President Rhee and his cabinet, MacArthur said:

"By the grace of a merciful Providence our forces fighting under the standard of that greatest hope and inspiration of mankind, the United Nations, have liberated this ancient capital of Korea. It has been freed from the despotism of Communist rule and its citizens once more [may be free] . . ."

Whereupon aged Syngman Rhee seized MacArthur's hand.

"We admire you," he said, tears filling his eyes. "We love you as the savior of our race."

Above: The U.N. drive back into Seoul resulted in some of the deadliest house-to-house street fighting of the war. Below: Marines cover a North Korean soldier emerging from a hole in a Seoul street. His clothing is afire.

The Chinese Trap

9

At United Nations headquarters in New York, the free-world nations rejoiced at the news of the stunning Inchon victory. They were hopeful that the knotty Korean problem would be solved at last. If the communist government of Premier Kim Il Sung could be driven out of the country, the way would be clear to hold free elections throughout all Korea.

In Korea itself, the ROKs of President Rhee started racing over the 38th Parallel in a dash for the North Korean-Chinese border along the Yalu River. General MacArthur also prepared to send his soldiers and marines across the Parallel. His men had mopped up most of the remnants of the shattered North Korean army below the line, and now the General was ready to send them farther north to complete the job. He had already received a directive from the Joint Chiefs authorizing movement north of the Parallel to carry out "destruction of the North Korean Armed Forces."

General MacArthur's plan to crush the North Korean armies and thus restore peace to the entire peninsula depended on coordinated attacks by two forces. On the west or left, facing north to the Yalu, was the Eighth Army under Bulldog Walker. On the east or right were the previously mentioned ROKs, as well as the First Marine Division and 7th Infantry Division, which made up X Corps under Major General Edward Almond. The joining of these two forces at the Yalu River would mean the end of Premier Kim Il Sung's army.

The Communists in the U.N. opposed such a

move. Premier Stalin even sent his foreign minister, Andrei Vishinsky, to New York for this purpose. At the Lake Success headquarters, Vishinsky calmly told the United Nations delegates that the 38th Parallel, which the North Korean Communists had already violated, was now a sacred line which the U.N. forces must not cross. The United Nations delegates were not impressed. On October 4, 1950, the General Assembly's Political and Security Committee voted to cross the Parallel and clear Korea for free elections. The vote was forty-seven to five, with seven nations abstaining.

Unfortunately the victory at Inchon had been so impressive and exciting that it led the United Nations—particularly the Americans—to miscalculate the intentions of Communist China. Late in September the Chinese foreign minister, Chou En-lai, had announced:

> The Chinese people absolutely will not tolerate foreign aggression, nor will they supinely tolerate seeing their neighbors savagely invaded by the imperialists.

Then on the night of October 1st, Chou called the Indian ambassador, K. M. Panikkar, to a dramatic midnight conference. During the course of their talk he told the Indian diplomat that China would enter the war if United States troops invaded North Korea. The news was relayed to President Truman, who has since written in his *Memoirs:*

> Similar reports had been received from Moscow, Stockholm, and New Delhi. However, the problem that arose in connection with these reports was that Mr. Panikkar had in the past played the game of the Chinese Communists fairly regularly, so that his statement could not be taken as that of an impartial observer. . . . The key vote on the [Korean] resolution was due the following day, and it appeared quite likely that Chou En-lai's "message" was a bald attempt to blackmail the United Nations by threats of intervention in Korea.

At MacArthur's headquarters, too, there was still a firm belief that the Chinese troops gathering along the Yalu would not enter the war. As the U.N. drive northward gathered speed, the watchword became "Home by Christmas."

On October 15th President Truman flew out

President Truman pins a Distinguished Service Medal with four oak leaf clusters on General MacArthur during ceremonies at Wake Island.

to Wake Island for a conference with General MacArthur. He pinned a fifth Distinguished Service Medal onto MacArthur's much beribboned blouse, and the General told him: "I believe that formal resistance will end throughout North Korea by Thanksgiving." The very next day the spearheads of 180,000 Red Chinese soldiers began stealing over the Yalu River.

One of the greatest abilities of the Chinese

Communist Forces (CCF) was that of being able to move great bodies of men secretly. The CCF was a peasant army; everybody marched on foot. There were not even many trucks to move supplies. The Chinese Reds had to rely on pack animals, including camels. Unluckily for the U.N., the rugged mountains of North Korea—on which the icy breath of a cruel winter was already beginning to fall—were made for such an army. Where the U.N. trucks might slip on icy roads or often become helplessly frozen, the Chinese Communist soldiers merely padded along on their canvas sneakers. Where U.N. columns were roadbound, the Communists could move overland. Moreover, in the mountains of North Korea there were many railroad tunnels and caves and mine shafts in which the communist armies could hide by day after having marched all night.

General Peng Teh-huai, who commanded the Chinese Communist Forces in Korea, had decided to make use of those mountains in his plan to trap and destroy the U.N. forces. First, he would achieve surprise by slipping his divisions over the Yalu in wanton disregard of interna-

tional law. Next, this force was to divide on either side of the mountain range, which also separated the U.N. Eighth Army from X Corps. Then the Chinese would strike without warning, pressing each of the U.N. forces against the sea, where they could be destroyed at leisure.

While the winter turned bitterly cold, General Peng Teh-huai bided his time, permitting the U.N. forces to move closer and closer to the jaws of his trap.

During those middle days of October, 1950, it seemed that the North Korean army had been crushed utterly. Everywhere resistance had crumbled. On the east the Rambling ROKs were sprinting for the border. The 1st Marine Division was preparing to land at Wonsan high in North Korea, and the 7th Infantry Division was sailing toward Iwon still higher north. There were fast-moving ROKs in the mountainous center, too, while on the west coast the Eighth Army swept all before it.

On October 19th patrols of the 1st Cavalry Division entered the enemy capital city of Pyong-

Soldiers of the Chinese Communist Forces hide out in a North Korean tunnel.

yang. They discovered that Premier Kim had fled, leaving behind him numerous paintings and busts of his mentor, Joseph Stalin. The riflemen pressed on, aided by the 24th Infantry Division, the British Commonwealth Brigade, the ROK 1st Division, and the paratroopers of the U.S. 187th Airborne Regiment—who jumped into action in an attempt to cut off the fleeing Reds.

Then began the mass surrender of the North Koreans. By the end of October 135,000 of them were in captivity, and Premier Kim's army had all but melted away. Kim himself was forced to flee farther northeast, hurrying right up to the Yalu River. On October 26th the ROK 7th Regiment reached the village of Chosan on the Yalu, and for all intents and purposes the war seemed over.

It was then that the Chinese Communist columns struck without warning.

Their first blows fell on those very ROK spearheads which had reached Chosan, the high point of the drive in the west. Two battalions from the ROK 2nd Regiment were annihilated in a sudden night attack, and then the ROK

7th Regiment was cut off and chopped up. Only 875 men of an original 3,552 escaped.

Thereafter, except for a three-week interval in November during which the Communists halted for supplies and reinforcements, Peng's commanders in the west threw in wave after wave of screaming, bugle-blatting troops in an attempt to pin the Eighth Army against the Yellow Sea. But Bulldog Walker and his officers and men kept their heads.

While Chou En-lai arrogantly boasted to the world that invincible Communist Chinese military power was going to hurl the U.N. out of all Korea, General Walker's divisions began to fall back in good order. Walker and MacArthur now understood the extent of the CCF's intervention in the Korean War. Realizing they were outnumbered, they decided to pull back to a line just below the 38th Parallel.

In this the U.N. was helped by the far-ranging planes of the U.S. Fifth Air Force and by the Corsairs and Pantherjets flown off carrier decks by Naval and Marine pilots. These war-birds hit the enemy whenever he dared to move along the roads in daylight. They helped the U.N. foot soldiers to fight and fall back, fight and fall back, leaving nothing but bullets and burned earth for the frantically onrushing enemy. In some places great red roaring bonfires were made of oil drums and other supplies which could not be moved, but which also could not be left for the enemy. In the end, General Peng Teh-huai failed to trap the Eighth Army. But he recklessly sacrificed thousands of men in his attempt to do so. The CCF was always ready to trade life for space.

Thus, on the west coast, the Chinese trap was eluded. But on the east, it looked as if the 1st Marine Division was doomed.

When the Chinese Communists first appeared in Korea, the U.N. X Corps forces in the east included two ROK divisions, the U.S. 7th Infantry Division, and the 1st Marine Division. The ROKs and the 7th Infantry were able to pull back quickly and begin a withdrawal on the port of Hungnam. But the 1st Marine Division continued its advance toward the Chosin Reser-

General Peng Teh-huai, commander of Chinese Communist Forces in Korea.

voir, seventy-eight miles northwest of Hungnam. This fitted right into the plans of General Sung Shin-lun, the fiery young commander who led the CCF in the east.

Sung wanted to wait until the marines got deep in the west and then cut them off. He intended to destroy the marines so that he could then rush into Hungnam and push the other U.N. forces against the Sea of Japan. Sung had his men ready. He had secretly moved 100,000 of them into position around Chosin Reservoir, a remarkable military feat for any commander.

The terrible cold winter weather of northeastern Korea had come early that year. And Sung was counting on it to deprive the marines of their accustomed speed. The freezing winter cut and slashed at men with cruel white claws. At night the temperature was down to twenty or thirty-five degrees below zero, and it rarely rose above zero during the day. Strong, knife-edged winds whipped frequent snowfalls into blizzards. In such extreme cold, weapons froze, food froze, human flesh and blood froze. The marines at Chosin had to run the motors of their vehicles every few hours to keep them from freezing. Weapons also had to be fired frequently for the same reason. Navy medical corpsmen, who take care of marines, had to put morphine Syrettes in their mouths to thaw them. And hungry men had also to thaw their frozen lumps of food before swallowing. If they did not, they would get terrible gnawing stomach pains. Frostbite was the common—and worst—danger. Sweat forming inside a marine's shoepac while he

A marine slogs through the stinging snow and ice.

marched or fought often froze and formed a sheath of ice around his foot as he slept.

In such frightful weather, moving through a barren land where a town or village was actually only a cluster of mud-thatched huts, the marines struck north. It was a fighting drive, and some of the enemy soldiers who were taken prisoner turned out to be Chinese. This alarmed Major General Oliver Smith of the 1st Marine Division. He suspected that there was a trap up north. But when he spoke of this to X Corps headquarters, he was told that his orders to march to Chosin could not be changed. Fortunately his request to build an airfield at a place called Hagaru-ri was granted. Work on it began just as the leading elements of General Smith's division reached a tiny hill town called Yudam-ni on the west or left of Chosin Reservoir.

Approximately 20,000 marines were drawing ever closer to General Sung's hidden horde of 100,000 Chinese soldiers. Worse, these marines were divided into four fragments stretched out for forty-one miles along the narrow winding road. One group was at Chinhung-ni thirty-

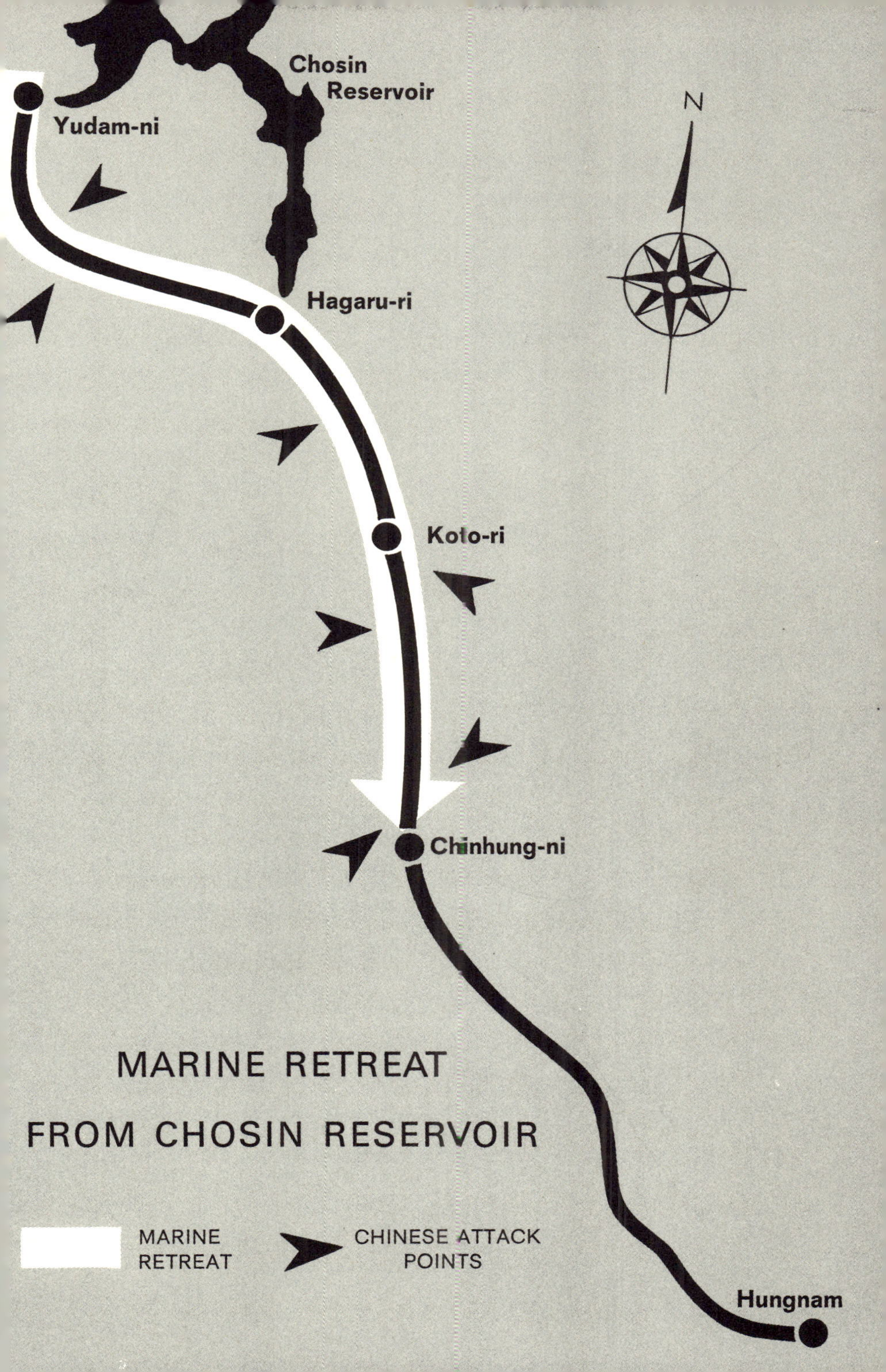

Chosin
Reservoir
Yudam-ni
N
Hagaru-ri
Koto-ri
Chinhung-ni
MARINE RETREAT
FROM CHOSIN RESERVOIR
MARINE
RETREAT
CHINESE ATTACK
POINTS
Hungnam

seven miles northwest of Hungnam. Another had reached Koto-ri, ten miles farther north, while a third—with General Smith and his headquarters—was eleven miles beyond at Hagaru-ri. The fourth group, the main body, had gotten to Yudam-ni, the most distant point of all. This fitted right into General Sung's plan for chopping up the Americans and destroying them piecemeal. He could send his ten divisions down both sides of the road to get in behind each of the towns held by the marines. In that way he would be able to cut the four groups off from each other.

When the Chinese struck in the west, putting the Eighth Army in mortal peril, the 1st Marine Division was ordered to attack west from Yudam-ni. This rescue effort also fell into General Sung's scheme. He wanted the Marine main body to advance west—into the jaws of his trap. Then he would cut them off. But the wary General Smith was still sniffing the Chosin air suspiciously. He ordered his Marine commanders at Yudam-ni—Lieutenant Colonel Raymond Murray and Colonel Homer Litzenberg—to proceed slowly.

This they did. And when they moved cautiously west on November 27th, they were not surprised to be struck suddenly by Red Chinese forces.

Murray and Litzenberg quickly pulled their men back to the Yudam-ni hills and began fortifying them. That night—to the blare of bugles, the shrill screaming of English profanity—the Communist Chinese attacked.

All night long the battle raged, a savage man-to-man kind of fighting during which soldiers grappled in the snow, rolling down the hills or struggling up them again, grenading and being grenaded. The hoarse battle shouts of the Americans mingled with the high cries of the Chinese. And over all this wild banshee screeching came the whuffling sound of mortar shells climbing into the night sky, and the thump and crash of the same shells striking the earth. In the morning the marines still held Yudam-ni. Two American regiments had beaten back two Chinese divisions.

United Nations forces to the east of Yudam-ni had not fared so well. There the Chinese assaulted a unit from the 7th Infantry Division and split it in two. This group—to be known as Task Force Faith—was doomed, although the gallant Colonel Don Faith who led it tried his best to bring his men out of the trap. Despite their valiant fighting, the task force fell apart. Many were taken prisoner, but many more were rescued off the ice of Chosin Reservoir by marines from Hagaru-ri.

The marines at Yudam-ni had made a gallant stand, but by the morning of November 28th General Sung's men had cut the road between all the towns and were busily fortifying the heights at either side of the road. Now the marines were not only surrounded; they were cut up into four separate groups. There was even a tiny fifth unit, far more important than its size. This was a company commanded by Captain William Barber; it held a high hill midway between Yudam-ni and Hagaru-ri. This height overlooked a narrow pass through which the Yudam-ni marines would have to move as they fought their way back to Hagaru-ri. If the Chinese captured the hill, they could mount artillery on it and cut the marines to bits. Captain Barber and his brave men held this hill for five days in the face of repeated attacks by forces ten times their number.

The height was still in American control when Murray and Litzenberg began blasting south to Hagaru-ri. So the Marine regiments got through the pass safely, though they had to fight almost every step of the way to Hagaru-ri. After they arrived at Hagaru-ri, they joined forces with General Smith's marines and soldiers, including a few hundred commandos of the Royal British Marines. Then they prepared to battle down to Koto-ri.

Just before they struck out, General Smith made a remark that was to become famous. War correspondents who had flown into the new airfield at Hagaru-ri—from which thousands of wounded marines had been evacuated—asked the General if it were true that United States Marines were retreating for the first time in history. General Smith replied:

"Gentlemen, we are not retreating. We are merely attacking in another direction."

And that was the truth, for the men of the

Major General Oliver Smith

1st Marine Division were taking a fearful toll of the enemy as they blasted through roadblock after roadblock, or stormed the hills lining the roads. Always they were helped by brother marines in the cockpits of low-flying Corsairs, or sometimes by planes of the Fifth Air Force, and occasionally by Australian pilots. And they did get into Koto-ri.

There the problems multiplied. Below Koto-ri was a bridge which the enemy had blown away and another narrow pass, this time beneath a height held by Chinese soldiers. But General Smith had used foresight. He had already arranged for the Fifth Air Force to air-drop bridge sections for spanning this gap, and had alerted a battalion at Chinhung-ni under Lieutenant Colonel Donald Schmuck to make a surprise attack on The Big Hill, as the height above the pass was called. The laying of the bridge and the surprise attack were to coincide.

Except for a very tense moment when a huge

Flames billow from an air-bombed Chinese roadblock erected to bar the way to marines withdrawing from Chosin Reservoir.

bulldozer caved in the new bridge, everything went off exactly on schedule. Colonel Schmuck's men marched north in a howling blizzard, bursting out of the snow to kill The Big Hill's defenders to a man. Then, as soon as the collapsed bridge was repaired, the huge eleven-mile-long column came winding out of Koto-ri. The marines next fought their way into Chinhung-ni, burst out of there, and finally marched down the mountainsides into the safety of the port at Hungnam, where the United States Navy was conducting a masterly evacuation.

Far from having been annihilated by General Sung's ten divisions, the 1st Marine Division had crippled the enemy. Although their casualties were 7,500—about half of these due to frostbite—the marines had inflicted approximately 37,500 casualties on the Communist Chinese.

Just before the movement from Koto, Colonel Murray had told his men: "We're going to take our dead, wounded, and equipment when we leave. We're coming out, I tell you, as Marines—or not at all."

That was how they came out.

The Second Retreat from Seoul

10

The Communist Chinese attack drastically altered the course of the war in Korea. Red China was now the open enemy of the United Nations, and little North Korea had been reduced to the status of a junior partner. From now on all the Communist battle tactics would be directed by the Chinese, chiefly by General Peng Teh-huai.

Moreover, a "Hate America Campaign" was in full froth in China and the United Nations itself was being attacked as the tool of "imperialist warmongers." The same sort of language was being echoed by the communist countries which were members of the U.N. organization. These countries still sought to block the U.N.'s attempt to bring peace to Korea. Why were they allowed to oppose the will of the vast majority of the United Nations?

The answer is simple. If the Russians and their satellites had left the United Nations, the world's hopes for a lasting peace would certainly have been doomed. Difficult though they were, these communist countries were at least still talking to the other nations and were thus subject to the criticism of world opinion. As Warren Austin, the United States ambassador to the United Nations, so aptly put it: "It is better for old men to talk to one another, than for young men to shoot at one another." Thus the United Nations made no attempt to silence the Russian Communists as they gave open support to their comrades in Communist China, a nation now boasting of how it was going to destroy the U.N. Command.

Confident of a Chinese victory, Russian dele-

Russian U.N. delegate Jacob Malik (left) raises his hand to indicate a veto of a six-power demand in the Security Council for the withdrawal of Chinese Communist troops from Korea.

gate Jacob Malik blocked United Nations attempts to negotiate with Red China. And Chou En-lai himself told the U.N. that he would not talk truce until the United Nations forces got out of Korea. In other words, there was no alternative but surrender. Chou's arrogance so angered the United Nations that all attempts to reason with Red China were dropped. President Truman instructed General MacArthur that his mission was now to deflate Communist China's inflated military pride.

That job, of course, would have fallen to Bulldog Walker. But the gallant leader of the Eighth Army was dead. He had lost his life in a highway accident, when a ROK truck rammed his jeep. The Eighth Army's new commander was a lieutenant general named Matthew Ridgway. Hawk-nosed and hard-muscled, General Ridgway was an inspiring leader. He was a paratrooper who had organized the 82nd Airborne Division—America's first paratroop outfit—and had led it on its first combat jump in Sicily. He also jumped with the division during the Normandy invasion.

The moment General Ridgway arrived in Korea he set himself to reviving the failing fighting spirit of his men. He put on his old paratrooper's jump harness—the grenade at the breast was to become his trademark—and drove straight to the front. Despite the freezing cold of that late December, 1950, he drove around the front for days, standing upright in an open jeep. He wanted the men to see him and take heart. They did, and soon he knew that the Eighth Army was solidly behind him.

One great boost for the morale of Ridgway's troops was the appearance of the swift American Sabrejets in Korea. For a time, the Russian-built MIG-15s had wrested fighter superiority in the air away from the slower-moving United States Shooting Stars. But on December 17th a flight of sleek Sabres led by Lieutenant Colonel Bruce Hinton went streaking up to the Yalu, where they were attacked by four MIGs. The enemy pilots came up boldly under the Sabres, perhaps thinking they had to deal with the slower Shooting Stars. The Sabres flashed down and Colonel Hinton's flaming guns sent a MIG spinning earthward in flames. It was the first MIG-15 destroyed in air-to-air combat. Thereafter the Sabres killed off Russia's best fighter plane at a rate of 14 to 1.

By this time, also, the Eighth Army had taken on a truly international flavor. All but a few of the sixteen nations committed to the Korean War had troops engaged, and these were trained in American battle tactics before being assigned to the eight United States divisions in Korea. The British formed the British Commonwealth Division out of troops from the United Kingdom, Canada, New Zealand and Australia.

Because of the different nationalities among the U.N. fighting forces, the supply officers did not have an easy time. Moslem Turks could not eat pork, and the Greeks did not like sweet potatoes, corn or peas. All European soldiers required extra bread, and those from the Mediterranean needed rations of olive oil. Oriental troops wanted only rice. Officers who thought to please them by giving them steak made a mistake, for the Orientals merely threw the steak in with the rice and boiled it. British troops wanted their tot of rum and the soldiers of the French Battalion wanted their glass of wine. Broader shoes had to be made for the Turks and the Greeks, and smaller sizes of all clothing had to be found for the Filipinos and Thailanders. But these were only some of the minor problems of the first U.N. army in history as the force of approximately a quarter-million men stood a little below

Members of a Turkish unit serving with U.N. forces in Korea raise their national colors at a camp behind the lines.

the 38th Parallel braced for the onslaught of about a half-million Chinese and North Koreans.

The attack began on New Year's Eve. All night long the Communist artillery and mortars bombarded the U.N. lines. Then, with the dawn of the New Year, 1951, seven CCF armies and two North Korean corps struck out for Seoul.

Throngs of battle-weary Korean civilians flee before the approaching Chinese Communist armies.

Although Chinese soldiers fell by the thousands, many thousands more swept on over frozen rice paddies and snowy hills. Large numbers of them were screaming, "Kill GI!"

Gradually the United Nations forces fell back, as Ridgway had planned to do. The Eighth Army commander knew he was outnumbered, but he had more guns. He wanted to keep drawing the onrushing enemy into his death-dealing artillery. And so a second U.N. retreat from Seoul was begun, while the British 29th Brigade and the U.S. 25th Division held the enemy north of the Han until everyone could be gotten safely out of the city. When this was done, General Ridgway himself took his departure. But before he left he found a pair of old pajamas with a hole in the seat of the trousers. These he tacked upon the wall of his headquarters with the following note beneath them:

TO THE COMMANDING GENERAL CHINESE COMMUNIST FORCES—WITH THE COMPLIMENTS OF THE COMMANDING GENERAL EIGHTH ARMY

The Road Back

11

Matthew Ridgway was a general who was not fond of retreat. After his Eighth Army and the ROKs had fallen back to a coast-to-coast line about sixty miles below the Parallel, he decided that the CCF advance might be slowing down. On January 15th he sent the 27th Wolfhounds probing north on an armored patrol.

The Wolfhounds rolled for about fifteen miles above Pyongtaek, passing through a frozen countryside in which the only signs of life were solitary civilians moving warily over frozen fields. Not until they reached Osan did the Wolfhounds encounter enemy soldiers. They exchanged rifle shots with them, and returned to report.

Ridgway was elated. The time had come for a counterstroke. Just to be sure, he went on a personal aerial scouting trip in a tiny two-seater plane flown by Lieutenant General Earle Partridge, the commander of the Fifth Air Force. For two hours they flew over a desolated land, seeing only an expanse of white snow, an occasional wisp of smoke from a hut that had escaped destruction, or footprints from villages to forests. The footprints suggested that the enemy was hiding out by day in the woods and sleeping in village huts by night. Obviously the CCF was neither numerous nor warlike.

So General Ridgway ordered his counterattack. It was halted momentarily by Chinese blows, but then it swept irresistibly forward. By mid-February the Communists were in full retreat. Hot to pursue, Ridgway ordered his famous Operation Killer, which drove the enemy back of the Han River. He followed this with Operation Ripper,

General Ridgway (center), the familiar grenade at his chest, personally surveys the front-line situation.

which brought about the second liberation of Seoul on March 14th.

Before the end of March the triumphant soldiers of the United Nations Command were once more crossing the 38th Parallel and punching into North Korea for distances of from ten to twenty miles. Ridgway and his men had done what President Truman and the United Nations desired them to do: they had burst the bubble of Chinese pride.

Then, with stunning suddenness, General Ridgway was ordered to Tokyo. A long-smoldering dispute between President Truman and General MacArthur had at last burst into flames. The President had relieved the General of all his commands and replaced him with Ridgway.

The disagreement between Mr. Truman and General MacArthur was as simple as it was drastic. The President wanted to fight a limited war in Korea because he feared that Premier Stalin hoped to get the United States bogged down there so that he could make further advances in Europe. General MacArthur believed that Communism's true goal was Asia, and he wished to extend the Korean War by bombing Communist China. There were other differences between them but this, basically, is what set them apart.

Since the beginning of the war there had been public signs of this difference, but in April, 1951, the affair came to a head. General MacArthur had sent a letter critical of the Truman Administration to a congressman, Representative Joseph Martin of Massachusetts. Representative

Martin read the letter on the floor of the House. President Truman took this as a challenge to his authority as commander in chief of America's armed forces. And so, on April 11, 1951, he dismissed General MacArthur.

Still ramrod-straight and handsome at seventy-one, General MacArthur returned to the United States. Many Americans felt that he was right, and that he had been mistreated. What was called "The Great Debate" followed between those Americans who wanted to extend the war in Korea and those who wanted to limit it. General MacArthur himself was given the rare privilege of addressing a joint session of Congress. During his historic farewell speech, he said:

"I am closing my fifty-two years of military service. When I joined the Army, even before the turn of the century, it was the fulfillment of all my boyish hopes and dreams. The world has turned over many times since I took the oath on the Plain at West Point, and the hopes and dreams have all since vanished.

"But I still remember the refrain of one of the most popular barracks ballads of that day, which proclaimed most proudly that old soldiers never die; they just fade away. And like the old soldier of that ballad, I now close my military career and just fade away, an old soldier who tried to do his duty as God gave him the light to see that duty. Good-by."

There were tears in the eyes of many congressmen, and of millions of Americans who watched the address on television, as they heard those final moving words from a great American soldier about to go into retirement. Even President Truman, despite their differences, said: "General MacArthur's place in history is firmly established."

In Korea, meanwhile, more history was being made. General Ridgway's promotion to Supreme Commander, U.N. Command, had brought the Eighth Army its third commanding officer in ten months—and he, like Ridgway, was a tiger.

Lieutenant General James Van Fleet came to Korea with an enviable record as a combat commander. A big, strong man—he had been a famous fullback for an undefeated Army football team—Van Fleet graduated from West Point in

1915. He was a member of that "class of the generals" which included Omar Bradley and Dwight Eisenhower. He had fought on the Mexican border, and during the First World War had been a machine-gun captain in France, where he was wounded. After that, Big Jim Van Fleet faded into obscurity, except for his reputation as a canny football coach at some of the colleges where he trained the R.O.T.C. But in the Second World War he came into his own, leading a regiment ashore at Normandy on D-Day. Then he took over a division and finally was promoted to command of a corps.

Following the war, he rebuilt the Greek army and directed the two-and-a-half-year war against guerrilla forces, stopping communist subversion there. Since Greece is a peninsula, the experience made Big Jim Van Fleet ably fitted for the peninsular warfare of Korea.

General Van Fleet took charge of the Eighth Army on April 14, 1951, barely a week before General Peng hurled half of his CCF and North Korean forces of 700,000 men against the U.N. battle line. Immediately Van Fleet ordered his

Lieutenant General James Van Fleet (left) confers with field commanders at an advanced command post near the front lines.

battle-wise divisions to give ground. They did, meanwhile plugging up gaps as they were opened by the enemy. Falling back below the Parallel, they bunched tighter together until at last they offered a solid front the Communists could not dent.

In the middle of May the Communists tried again, once more boasting that they would drive the United Nations into the sea. This time they were cut to ribbons by the famous "Van Fleet Load," an unprecedented volume of artillery fire which was five times the normal output.

"We must expend steel and fire, not men," said Van Fleet. "I want so many artillery holes that a man can step from one to the other."

And so the Van Fleet Load went howling through the night toward twenty-one Chinese and nine North Korean divisions. The result was a terrible slaughter. One United States artillery battalion alone fired 12,000 shells in a single day. Still the CCF commanders forced their men on, caring nothing about how many lives the advance would cost. All they wanted was to get into Seoul again.

But there was to be no third U.N. retreat from Seoul. Rather, there was to be a third United Nations crossing of the 38th Parallel. This time the U.N. advance was so savage and so destructive of Chinese Communist hopes that even their Russian comrades in the United Nations stopped echoing Chinese boasts and suddenly began to plead for a truce.

This turnabout came on June 23rd. United

A Yank soldier holds his bayonet-tipped rifle at the ready as he moves cautiously into a wrecked house during the third U.N. drive into North Korea.

Nations Secretary General Trygve Lie had already publicly stated that the time to talk peace had come. But there had been no reply from the Russians until, on the twenty-third, Soviet delegate Jacob Malik appeared on the United Nations weekly radio broadcast. He spent a quarter-hour in customary abuse of the United States. Then, talking overtime, he said:

"The Soviet peoples further believe that the most acute problem of the present day—the problem of the armed conflict in Korea—could also be settled. This would require the readiness of the parties to enter on the path of peaceful settlement of the Korean question. The Soviet peoples believe that as a first step discussions should be started between the belligerents for a cease-fire and an armistice providing for the mutual withdrawal of forces from the 38th Parallel."

Two days later the Chinese Communists seconded Malik's proposal. On June 29, 1951, General Ridgway broadcast this message to the Communist enemy:

"I am informed that you may wish a meeting

to discuss an armistice . . .

"Upon the receipt of word from you that such a meeting is desired I shall be prepared to name my representative. I propose that such a meeting could take place aboard a Danish hospital ship *(Jutlandia)* in Wonsan Harbor."

The following night Premier Kim Il Sung and General Peng Teh-huai agreed to the meeting, but they suggested it take place in the town of Kaesong about a mile below the Parallel and ten miles northwest of the U.N. west flank. Ridgway accepted this counter-offer, and the famous—and incredible—"truce talks" began.

The Truce Talks Drag On

12

To the soldiers of the U.N. forces in Korea there would never be a stranger or more puzzling period than the two years which followed the beginning of the truce talks at Kaesong.

At first it seemed that the end of mud and misery was in sight. Only gradually did the troops understand that as yet there was no actual truce—just an agreement to *talk* about a truce. Meanwhile the fighting would continue.

The Communists at Kaesong talked loudly about wanting the fighting to stop, but this was only because the U.N. was now on the offensive. The Eighth Army and the ROKs stood well inside the territory of North Korea and had the power to advance farther. More, United Nations sea and air power—almost completely American—was able to do as it pleased in the waters around Korea and the air above it. The Communists proceeded to demand that the U.N. agree to an immediate cease-fire and a withdrawal below the 38th Parallel. But if the U.N. had agreed to such a demand it would have been giving up the very advantage which had caused the Communists to ask for truce talks.

The talks, which began at a teahouse in Kaesong on July 10th, dragged on for another twenty-four months. Meanwhile both armies settled down to a trench warfare of the kind fought in World War I. It was a complete turnabout in battlefield tactics. The wild marching and counter-marching up and down the peninsula, characteristic of the first year of the war—"The Shooting War"—now settled down to the stalemate and irregular flare-ups of "The Talking War."

In The Talking War, almost every battle was fought to influence the truce talks. The Communists, believing in nothing but power, only agreed to certain things after their own attempts to beat down the U.N. advantage were broken up, or after the U.N. pushed them back a few more miles. Such fighting was very hard for young soldiers to understand. Thus it was all the more to the credit of those American soldiers and their allies that they fought on.

Propaganda guns had been blasting away from the moment the Communists agreed to talk. The Chinese and North Korean people were told that the American "paper tigers" were begging for peace. When Colonel Andrew Kinney led a U.N. advance party to "neutral" Kaesong, he found the town was a Communist armed camp. His men were required to fly white flags from their jeeps so that crowds of Communist correspondents and cameramen would have proof that the U.N. was on its knees. On the very first day of the meetings, Admiral C. Turner Joy, the

U.N. senior delegate, had to push aside a burp gun which an arrogant Communist soldier pointed at him. Another insolent guard told Colonel Kinney that the medal on his chest was "for killing forty Americans." Next, when Admiral Joy sat down, he found that the legs of his chair had been sawed off so that he was made to seem smaller than little Lieutenant General Nam Il. This, also, was photographed as proof of Communist superiority.

Nam Il was the leader of the North Korean delegation. He was slender, smooth-faced, and natty in a gaudy uniform with striped breeches and gleaming leather boots. Major General Chang Pyong San and Lee Sang Cho of the North Korean army were also present, but the real chief of the Communist delegation was Chinese General Hseih Fang, a lean, bony man with a keen mind and sharp tongue. Even Nam Il would glance at Hseih before beginning to speak.

On Admiral Joy's team of negotiators were Major General L. C. Craigie, Major General Henry Hodes, and Rear Admiral Arleigh ("Thirty-one Knot") Burke—all Americans.

From the moment these two teams met, the truce talks became a bitter wrangle. The Communists opened the meeting by coolly demanding that the United Nations forces withdraw below the 38th Parallel. Admiral Joy refused, and the angry arguing continued until August 22nd.

On that date the Communists accused the U.N. of bombing Kaesong and trying to murder their delegation. It made no difference that Colonel Kinney, himself an aviator, could find not a

The U.N. delegation at the cease-fire talks held in Kaesong. Left to right: Major General Henry Hodes, Major General L. C. Craigie, Vice Admiral C. Turner Joy, Major General Paik Sun Yup, and Rear Admiral Arleigh A. Burke.

shred of evidence that Kaesong had been bombed. Nor were the Communists bothered by the fact that the "bomb" they produced was actually an outmoded American rocket which had not been issued to U.N. fliers for nearly a year. They continued to broadcast their charges to the world, and an exasperated General Ridgway replied by breaking off the truce talks.

After the rest of the world had refused to accept the "Kaesong bombing" hoax, the Communists sent approximately a million men plunging south against the force of 586,000 troops commanded by Lieutenant General Van Fleet. The attack was stopped dead, and Van Fleet then sent the 229,000 men of his Eighth Army and 357,000 ROKs battling north on a drive of their own. As a result the Communists lost more ground. In the middle of October, 1951, they agreed to return to the conference table. This time the talks were at a place called Panmunjom. General Ridgway had had enough of Kaesong. But at Panmunjom the war-weary world's hopes for peace seemed dashed again—this time on the problem of prisoner return.

Members of the North Korean truce team at Panmunjom. Left to right: Colonel Chang, Rear Admiral Kim Won Mu, General Lee Sang Cho, General Nam Il, General Hseih Fang, Colonel Tsai.

The Korean War had shown the world many new things, but nothing so startling as the spectacle of 60,000 captured Chinese and North Korean soldiers refusing to go home. They not only refused to return, but asked the United Nations to prevent their being forced to do so.

This stung the Communist World more deeply than the actual loss of ten or a hundred times that many men in battle. Such a mass rejection disproved all the Communists' claims about the superiority of their own way of life. That is why, for eighteen months after the renewal of talks at Panmunjom, the Communist negotiators stubbornly refused to accept what was called "voluntary repatriation." This meant that no captured soldier of either side could be made to go home against his will. It was given determination by President Truman's remark: "We will not buy an armistice by turning over human beings for slaughter or slavery."

There were other issues on which the two sides at Panmunjom disagreed, but all of them were secondary to this big one. And all the secondary problems were eventually worked out. But on the matter of prisoner return, the Communists said, in effect: "We want all of our captured soldiers returned to us, at bayonet point if necessary."

Their intent was to discredit the U.N. Command—particularly the United States leadership—and thus prove that the 60,000 soldiers who refused to come home were actually being held against their will. The first move was to organize a prison riot on the big island of Koje, about twenty miles southwest of Pusan. There were 150,000 prisoners of war (POWs) on Koje, housed in huge compounds holding approximately 6,000 men each. And there were very few guards because troops were badly needed to hold the battlefront.

Into these compounds the Communists smuggled men who had been trained in sabotage and then ordered to surrender to the U.N. Gradually, under the command of a North Korean colonel, Lee Hak Koo, the Red prisoners took secret control of the compounds. They set up unauthorized "courts" and passed death sentences on fellow prisoners who seemed friendly to the United Nations. Execution was carried out by beating the men to death with tent poles, while the Communists drowned out their screams by howling patriotic songs.

Next, they built an arsenal. Oil drums used as garbage cans were converted into primitive forges in which crude knives, swords, hatchets and bayonets were made. Steel arch supports from GI shoes were fashioned into spearheads

A North Korean prisoner, injured in the bloody compound riot, is led to the hospital for treatment.

fitted to the tips of poles. Cruel flails were made by fitting strips of barbed wire to wooden handles, and gunpowder was manufactured from wood ashes and crude nitrates extracted from urine. When United Nations interrogators appeared at Koje in February to ask who wished to go home and who wished to stay, the Red-led cells rose in a bloody riot. The 27th Wolfhounds were called in to quell the uprising. Although given orders not to shoot, they were forced to defend themselves when the Reds charged. The riot was put down with American casualties of one dead and thirty-nine wounded, as opposed to seventy-five prisoners dead and one hundred and thirty-nine wounded.

General Nam Il at Panmunjom, who had plotted the entire uprising, now had the verbal ammunition he needed. He accused the United Nations of "massacring" captured prisoners. "In order to cover up this fact," he said, "your side has invented the myth that our captured personnel were not willing to be repatriated."

The final blow to U.N. prestige was the Communists' capture of the Koje commandant, Brigadier General Francis Dodd. They held him for ransom until Brigadier General Charles Colson unwisely signed a pledge to cease "violence and bloodshed" among the prisoners of war. It was not true, of course, but General Nam Il *really* had ammunition now. "Is it a sign of your good faith," he asked, "to continue to slaughter war prisoners in open repudiation of the pledge of no further maltreatment or murder of war prisoners made by Colson?"

Finally General Van Fleet ordered Brigadier General Haydon Boatner to break the Communist hold on Koje. Boatner's men went in hurling tear-gas grenades and shattered the Red grip in a brief fight. When the Red compounds were searched, the skeletons of sixteen prisoners executed by the mock courts were unearthed.

The Communists next attempted to smear the United Nations by a "germ warfare hoax." According to the Chinese Reds, the United States Air Force had waged germ warfare by dropping canisters filled with deadly typhus germs on North Korea. The truth of the matter was that the Chinese themselves had introduced typhus

Communist prisoners file past U.N. guards, who wear masks to protect them against tear gas used to subdue rebellious POWs.

into North Korea when their men crossed the Yalu from typhus-ridden Manchuria. But the Communists were able to give "proof" to their charges by obtaining "confessions" to germ warfare from captured American airmen.

The method of extracting these so-called confessions was simple torture. For instance, one American flier was ordered to "confess" eight times under penalty of death. He was kept standing at attention for five hours at a time and confined for eight days in a doorless cell less than six feet long. He was held to the ground while a guard kicked and slapped him, then ordered to stand at attention for twenty-two hours until he fell over. While lying down, he was struck on the head with the flat of a hatchet. His tormentors questioned him for three hours with a spotlight held six inches from his face, then ordered him to confess while a pistol was held at the back of his head. He was placed under a roof drain all night during a rainstorm, then left without food for three days. And finally he was put before a firing squad, then given a last chance and hung alternately by his hands and feet from the rafters of a house. Throughout all this, the American refused to confess. The Communists at last tired of this unyielding prisoner and left him alone.

But there were others subjected to the same torture who were not so strong. Even though these prisoners repudiated their "confessions" after the war ended, it was a long time before the truth finally caught up with the germ warfare hoax. Yet, the United Nations, led by the United States, refused to budge from its stand against forced return of prisoners.

This stand was maintained throughout the changes in command which the American presidential election of 1952 brought to Korea. After General Dwight Eisenhower resigned his command of the North Atlantic Treaty Organization to make his successful campaign for the Presidency, General Ridgway took his place in France. General Mark Clark came to Tokyo to become U.N. Supreme Commander. Then, in April of 1953, after General Van Fleet had reached retirement age, the command of the Eighth Army was given to General Maxwell Taylor. Meanwhile, Admiral Joy turned over his position as senior delegate at Panmunjom to Lieutenant General William Harrison. But the stand against forced repatriation of prisoners was not changed. President Eisenhower himself said:

"To force those people to go back to a life of terror and persecution is something that would violate every moral standard by which America lives. Therefore, it would be unacceptable to the American code, and it cannot be done."

And so, with all truce talks broken off, the war dragged on. Every night soldiers and marines blacked their faces and stole out on patrols into the no man's land between themselves and the Chinese. Occasionally battles erupted between forces that, in the spring of 1953, stood at 768,000 men on the United Nations side and a little more than a million for the Communists. But for the most part the war was a stalemate of the dreariest kind, and the outlook for its end was very bleak indeed. Then, on March 5, 1953, the following announcement was broadcast over the Moscow radio:

"The heart of the comrade and inspired continuer of Lenin's will, the wise leader and teacher of the Communist Party and the Soviet People—Josef Vissarionovich Stalin—has stopped beating."

The Communist world was turned upside down! Stalin's death brought a change in the Soviet attitude toward Korea. Soon even the Communist Chinese, free now of the iron hand which had certainly helped push them into the war, began asking for renewal of the truce talks. On March 28 Chou En-lai began to soften his stand slightly on the prisoner return issue. And in April both sides exchanged their sick and wounded prisoners. By the end of that month the two teams of negotiators returned to the green-topped table at Panmunjom, and the world began to hope aloud that the war would actually end at last.

Everyone, that is, except South Korea's President Syngman Rhee.

Korea's "grand old man" had a single passionate purpose in life. That was to see his country free and united. To him a truce with the Communists was unthinkable. It would mean that his country would continue to be separated into the states of South and North Korea, and Communism would remain on his borders. Worse, the Communist Chinese, whom he hated, would remain in charge on that border.

For this reason, whenever both sides at Panmunjom showed signs of agreement, Syngman Rhee did or said something to drive a wedge between them. Finally, when the closest agreements of all were being made in May of 1953, Rhee openly announced his opposition to a truce. He said that he would continue the war on his own, if necessary. On June 18th he nearly scuttled the armistice for good when, without warning, his guards freed 27,000 North Koreans held as prisoners of war, and smuggled them into the hills and private homes of South Korea.

The Communists were outraged and broke off the talks. All hopes were once again dashed and everything looked as black as before. But then President Eisenhower made sweeping offers of help for Rhee's poverty-stricken country, and

the stubborn old president at last consented to support the armistice.

The last details were worked out, with the Communists agreeing that no prisoner need go home if he did not want to. In all, about 50,000 Chinese and North Korean soldiers finally refused to return to communism, while only about 350 South Koreans, 23 American soldiers, and 1 Briton initially seemed to prefer communism. This was a grave blow to the cause of world communism.

It was also agreed that after the armistice there should be a peace conference in Geneva for the purpose of finally settling the Korean problem.

At ten o'clock in the morning of July 27, 1953, Lieutenant General William Harrison and Lieutenant General Nam Il silently led their delegations into the Panmunjom "peace pagoda" of tar paper and straw mat. They sat at a straight row of tables to sign the eighteen copies of the Armistice Agreement, nine of these bound in United Nations blue, nine of them in Communist red. Ten minutes later they arose and walked out. They had said not a single word to each other. In another twelve hours, the guns fell silent all over the peninsula. The Korean War was over.

The Fighting Ends

13

There never was a peace conference to settle the Korean problem. The Communists had no intention of running the risks of free elections throughout the peninsula. And since a free and united Korea had been the original goal of the United Nations, the world organization was unwilling to accept anything less.

So the armistice agreement ended nothing but the shooting. The state of war which is concluded with the customary signing of a peace treaty did not officially end. Two armies continued to face each other in Korea in a state of "armed truce." In 1963 approximately 1,500,000 men in the forces of Red China and Communist North Korea confronted a South Korean army of 500,000 men, reinforced by two American divisions. The South Korean force occupied the final position of the U.N. Command above the Parallel—a defense line much easier to defend than the old one violated by the Communists. Between them and the Communists stretched a two-and-a-half-mile no man's land, or Demilitarized Zone, provided under the armistice agreement.

Was the United Nations crusade in Korea, then, a failure?

No. Those sixteen nations that rallied to fight for freedom in Korea showed the world that the notion of nobility is not dead. For three years they fought to uphold a country's right to choose its own way of life. Nothing on such a scale had ever happened before. The Korean War is the first war in history in which troops of a

Two Americans patrol the demilitarized zone separating North and South Korea.

world organization—the United Nations—acted as a "police force" to fight an aggressor nation.

Bibliographical Note

Younger readers who find the Korean War so interesting that they may wish to go beyond this book will find it difficult to come across many complete adult works on the subject. So far as I know there are two: *This Kind of War* by T. R. Ferenbaugh, The Macmillan Company, 1963, and my own *Conflict: The History of the Korean War,* G. P. Putnam's Sons, 1962 (paperback edition: Avon Book Division of the Hearst Corporation). There are, however, numerous works on various aspects of the war. Some of these are listed below:

Cagle, Malcolm W., and Manson, Frank A., *The Sea War in Korea.* Annapolis: United States Naval Institute, 1957. (A clear and complete account of the United Nations at sea.)

Clark, General Mark W., *From the Danube to the Yalu.* New York: Harper and Row, Publishers, 1954. (The third United Nations Commander relates his conduct of the war and tells of his difficult negotiations with South Korean President Syngman Rhee.)

Dean, Major General William F., *General Dean's Story.* New York: The Viking Press, 1954. (A vivid and gripping account of General Dean's heroic delaying action, the defeat at Taejon, his capture and ordeal in the hands of the Chinese Communists.)

Donovan, Robert J., *Eisenhower, the Inside Story.* New York: Harper and Row, Publishers, 1956. (A narrative of President Dwight D. Eisenhower's first few years of office which includes a description of his difficult relations with President Syngman Rhee and the conclusion of the truce.)

Gugeler, Captain Russell A., *Combat Actions in Korea.* Washington: Combat Forces Press, 1954. (An instructive collection of eyewitness accounts of the fighting.)

Joy, Admiral C. Turner, *How Communists Negotiate.* New York: The Macmillan Company, 1955. (A valuable lesson in the tactics employed by the Communists at the conference table, given by the chief of the U.N. delegation to the truce talks.)

Poats, Rutherford M., *Decision in Korea.* New York: The Robert M. McBride Company, Inc., 1954. (Swift-moving outline of the war with particular attention paid to the first six months.)

Ridgway, General Matthew B., *Soldier: The Memoirs of Matthew B. Ridgway.* New York: Harper and Row, Publishers, 1956. (Some of General Ridgway's passages dealing with the course of the war, his own conduct as commander of the Eighth Army and later as United Nations Commander are among the most lucid and compelling of Korean War literature.)

Russ, Martin, *The Last Parallel.* New York: Rinehart and Winston, Inc., 1957. (A young Marine's war diary which provides insights into the character of the fighting.)

Truman, Harry S., *Memoirs by Harry S. Truman,* Vol. II, *Years of Trial and Hope.* Garden City: Doubleday and Company, Inc., 1956. (President Truman's own account of his actions during the first two years of the war.)

White, W. L., *The Captives of Korea.* New York: Charles Scribner's Sons, 1957. (A detailed, sometimes humorous account of the prisoner exchange, as well as of the germ-warfare hoax.)

Index

About the Author

ROBERT LECKIE was a scout and machine-gunner with the First Marine Division during World War II, and was awarded the Naval Commendation Medal for action at Peleliu. His first book, *Helmet for My Pillow,* is a narrative of his war experiences; in 1957 it won the annual award of the Marine Corps Combat Correspondents Association.

Two of Mr. Leckie's subsequent books are about the Korean War: *The March to Glory* and *Conflict.* The latter is the first full-scale history of the war to be published. It was hailed by New York *Times* critic Orville Prescott as "so complete, authoritative, lively and readable that it establishes Mr. Leckie as one of our foremost military historians." The author has also written three adventure books for boys, as well as numerous short stories and articles for national magazines.

Born in Philadelphia and raised in Rutherford, New Jersey, Mr. Leckie has had wide newspaper and film experience. He has worked on eight newspapers as a reporter, sports writer, financial editor, and copy editor. Formerly the editor of MGM's theater newsreel, he has also written documentary films and edited *The Telenews Weekly.* Mr. Leckie, his wife and three children live in Mountain Lakes, New Jersey.

World Landmark Books

W-1 The First Men in the World *by Anne Terry White*
W-2 Alexander the Great *by John Gunther*
W-3 Adventures and Discoveries of Marco Polo *by Richard J. Walsh*
W-4 Joan of Arc *by Nancy Wilson Ross*
W-5 King Arthur and His Knights *by Mabel Louise Robinson*
W-6 Mary, Queen of Scots *by Emily Hahn*
W-7 Napoleon and the Battle of Waterloo *by Frances Winwar*
W-8 Royal Canadian Mounted Police *by Richard L. Neuberger*
W-9 The Man Who Changed China: The Story of Sun Yat-sen *by Pearl S. Buck*
W-10 The Battle of Britain *by Quentin Reynolds*
W-11 The Crusades *by Anthony West*
W-12 Genghis Khan and the Mongol Horde *by Harold Lamb*
W-13 Queen Elizabeth and the Spanish Armada *by Frances Winwar*
W-14 Simon Bolivar, the Great Liberator *by Arnold Whitridge*
W-15 The Slave Who Freed Haiti: The Story of Toussaint Louverture *by Katharine Scherman*
W-16 The Story of Scotland Yard *by Laurence Thompson*
W-17 The Life of Saint Patrick *by Quentin Reynolds*
W-19 Captain Cook Explores the South Seas *by Armstrong Sperry*
W-20 Marie Antoinette *by Bernardine Kielty*
W-21 Will Shakespeare and the Globe Theater *by Anne Terry White*
W-22 The French Foreign Legion *by Wyatt Blassingame*
W-23 Martin Luther *by Harry Emerson Fosdick*
W-24 The Hudson's Bay Company *by Richard Morenus*
W-25 Balboa: Swordsman and Conquistador *by Felix Riesenberg, Jr.*

W-26 The Magna Charta *by James Daugherty*
W-27 Leonardo da Vinci *by Emily Hahn*
W-28 General Brock and Niagara Falls *by Samuel Hopkins Adams*
W-29 Catherine the Great *by Katharine Scherman*
W-30 The Fall of Constantinople *by Bernardine Kielty*
W-31 Ferdinand Magellan: Master Mariner *by Seymour Gates Pond*
W-32 Garibaldi: Father of Modern Italy *by Marcia Davenport*
W-33 The Story of Albert Schweitzer *by Anita Daniel*
W-34 The Marquis de Lafayette: Bright Sword of Freedom *by Hodding Carter*
W-35 Famous Pirates of the New World *by A. B. C. Whipple*
W-36 Exploring the Hamalaya *by William O. Douglas*
W-37 Queen Victoria *by Noel Streatfeild*
W-38 The Flight and Adventures of Charles II *by Charles Norman*
W-39 Chief of the Cossacks *by Harold Lamb*
W-40 Adventures of Ulysses *by Gerald Gottlieb*
W-41 William the Conqueror *by Thomas B. Costain*
W-42 Jesus of Nazareth *by Harry Emerson Fosdick*
W-43 Julius Caesar *by John Gunther*
W-44 The Story of Australia *by A. Grove Day*
W-45 Captain Cortés Conquers Mexico *by William Johnson*
W-46 Florence Nightingale *by Ruth Fox Hume*
W-47 The Rise and Fall of Adolf Hitler *by William L. Shirer*
W-48 The Story of Atomic Energy *by Laura Fermi*
W-49 Great Men of Medicine *by Ruth Fox Hume*
W-50 Cleopatra of Egypt *by Leonora Hornblow*
W-51 The Sinking of the Bismarck *by William L. Shirer*
W-52 Lawrence of Arabia *by Alistair MacLean*
W-53 The Life of Saint Paul *by Harry Emerson Fosdick*
W-54 The Voyages of Henry Hudson *by Eugene Rachlis*
W-55 Hero of Trafalgar *by A. B. C. Whipple*
W-56 Winston Churchill *by Quentin Reynolds*
W-57 The War in Korea: 1950–53 *by Robert Leckie*
W-58 Walter Raleigh *by Henrietta Buckmaster*
W-59 The Pharaohs of Ancient Egypt *by Elizabeth Payne*
W-60 Flying Aces of World War I *by Gene Gurney*
W-61 The Commandos of World War II *by Hodding Carter*